T0150931

Printed in the USA
CPSIA information can be obtained
at www.ICGtesting.com
JSHW030307170823
46715JS00002B/6

9 781646 053032

Rawley Grau is best known as a translator from Russian and Slovenian. His translation of the Russian poet Yevgeny Baratynsky (*A Science Not for the Earth*, 2015) received the AATSEEL Prize for Best Scholarly Translation and was listed by *Three Percent* as one of the ten best poetry translations of the year. His translations from Slovenian of two novels by Dušan Šarotar (*Panorama*, 2017, and *Billiards at the Hotel Dobray*, 2019) were shortlisted for the Oxford-Weidenfeld Prize. In 2021, he was awarded the Lavrin Diploma for excellence in translation by the Slovenian Association of Literary Translators. Originally from Baltimore, he has lived in Ljubljana, Slovenia, since the early 2000s.

Christina E. Kramer is a professor emerita at the University of Toronto, Canada, where she taught Macedonian for more than thirty years. She is the author of numerous articles on Balkan linguistics as well as a Macedonian grammar. Her translations include *Fear of Barbarians* by Petar Andonovski (Parthian Press, 2022); *A Spare Life* by Lidija Dimkovska (Two Lines Press, 2016, longlisted for Best Translated Book of the year); *Freud's Sister* by Goce Smilevski (Penguin Books, 2012, Lois Roth Prize Honourable Mention); and three novels by Luan Starova: *My Father's Books* and *The Time of the Goats* (both University of Wisconsin Press, 2012), and *The Path of the Eels* (supported by an NEA grant; Autumn Hill Books, 2017). For additional information: www.christinakramertranslator.ca.

ABOUT THE CONTRIBUTORS

Aco Šopov was born in 1923 in the city of Štip in what is today North Macedonia. His first book was published by the underground press near the end of World War II, in which he had fought as a Partisan in the anti-fascist resistance. By the early 1950s, he was a major Macedonian poet. His books *Not-Being* (*Nebidnina,* 1963) and *Reader of the Ashes* (*Gledač vo pepelta,* 1970) are genuine masterworks, consolidating his reputation as one of the founders of modern Macedonian poetry. Šopov's poetic mission was to develop a poetry rooted in his own culture and language that is also universal and modern, and to do this not by turning away from tradition but by drawing on something that is both of the moment yet beyond the realm of time. This creative yet destructive impulse, which lies at the core of being, he called "the fire." His health began to decline in the late 1970s, and he died in 1982, at the age of fifty-eight. Šopov's work has been translated into over a dozen languages. This bilingual collection, which marks the poet's centennial, is the first major edition of Šopov's poetry in English.

Jasmina Šopova, a journalist, translator, and editor, was until recently the longtime editor-in-chief of the quarterly magazine *The UNESCO Courier,* where she published articles and interviews with Enki Bilal, René Depestre, Édouard Maunick, Predrag Matvejević, and other writers and artists from France, the Caribbean, Africa, and Southeastern Europe. She has translated the poets Adonis and Mahmoud Darwish from French into Macedonian and the Macedonian poets Ante Popovski, Vlada Uroševik, and Aco Šopov (her father) into French. She is the author of a number of monographs and critical editions in the field of poetry. As the vice-president of the Aco Šopov Poetry Foundation, she manages the foundation's multilingual website devoted to her father's life and work (www.acosopov.com).

PRAISE FOR ACO ŠOPOV

"What particularly attracts me in the poetry of Aco Šopov, what so profoundly moves me, is the way he listens—patiently, ceaselessly and very lucidly—to what he calls 'the blood.' This is not the blood of vendetta, civil war, or conflict. It is the blood of the great Shakespearean drama of life. It is the blood of the word, of the ceaseless heartbeat of the human space." —Yves Bergeret, poet

"A Šopov poem awakens the perfumes, the indefinable sap of his country, in other words, that reality which is both tangible and intangible, for the sake of which one sometimes dies." —Pierre Seghers, poet

"Rawley Grau and Christina E. Kramer's translations of Aco Šopov's lyrics reproduce the remarkable clarity and depth of this Macedonian master's vision, a vision hardened like a diamond by the forces of private and public catastrophe. In these incantatory lines, strikingly stark images of the natural world blend with revelatory reflections on and from the human interior. Šopov keeps our eyes and our minds focused on the eternal chiaroscuro of existence. Time and again, he dazzles us with 'those flashes of lightning that sleep in darkness.'"
—Boris Dralyuk, poet and translator

"Aco Šopov was like a literary aristocrat who took poetry as his adoptive sister, his only accomplice, his only confidant. The purity of his poetic language, especially in his second phase of literary creation, rivals that of the masterpieces of Central European literature." —Gane Todorovski, poet

"Aco Šopov gives us the fire smoldering in the roots of trees, in the black sun, in the silence before the poem is composed. These poems burn with old fires, medieval battle cries, primordial limestone. This is a book for spelunkers and myth-makers. Grau and Kramer translate with the strength of blacksmiths working iron. The fire in these poems has been coming for a long time, indeed. I'm glad it's here."
—Sean Cotter, translator of *Solenoid* and *FEM*

ACO ŠOPOV

The Long Coming of the Fire

Selected Poems

——

COMPILED BY JASMINA ŠOPOVA

TRANSLATED FROM THE MACEDONIAN
BY RAWLEY GRAU AND CHRISTINA E. KRAMER

PHONEME
MEDIA

DEEP
VELLUM

DALLAS, TEXAS

Phoneme Media, an imprint of Deep Vellum Publishing
3000 Commerce St., Dallas, Texas 75226

Deep Vellum is a 501c3 nonprofit literary arts organization founded in 2013 with the mission to bring the world into conversation through literature.

Support for this publication has been provided in part by grants from the National Endowment for the Arts, the Texas Commission on the Arts, the City of Dallas Office of Arts and Culture, the George and Fay Young Foundation, the Aco Šopov Poetry Foundation, Nova Generation, and the United Macedonian Diaspora.

This translation is published with the financial support of the Ministry of Culture of the Republic of North Macedonia.

Република Северна Македонија
Министерство за култура

Republika e Maqedonisë së Veriut
Ministria e Kulturës

978-1-64605-303-2 (paperback) | 978-1-64605-318-6 (ebook)

LIBRARY OF CONGRESS CATALOGING NUMBER: 2023031348

Cover design by Chad Felix

Interior layout and typesetting by KGT

PRINTED IN THE UNITED STATES OF AMERICA

CONTENTS

NOT-BEING (1963)

READER OF THE ASHES (1970)

EARLIER POEMS

LATER POEMS

APPENDIX: ACO ŠOPOV ON THE SKOPJE EARTHQUAKE OF 1963

Looking Up at the Perfect Silence of the Stars

Jasmina Šopova

Now, for the first time, English speakers will have the opportunity to become acquainted with a Macedonian poet from the past century who is nevertheless very much our contemporary: Aco Šopov, my father.

Although he was born a hundred years ago, I call him our contemporary—and I believe he will also be the contemporary of future generations—because his poetry, at its most fundamental, knows neither temporal nor geographic boundaries.

"In Aco Šopov's poetry no one feels a stranger," the Egyptian writer Mahmoud Hussein wrote two decades ago. Those who read his poetry cannot help but recognize themselves in it, to the degree that they have been able to make their way along its enigmatic meanderings. Of course, mystery would not be one of the fundamental attributes of poetry if the poetic word stood before us stripped bare.

I have taken the liberty of adapting a line from Walt Whitman for the title of this foreword about a poet whose verses on silence are well known throughout his country. To me, my father's silence is the silence of the stars. From out of that cosmic silence emerged his word, which sings of itself and through which the poet sings of himself, while, at the same time, being "the word En-Masse."

Šopov, I think, was among those who are called by the menacing voice of the "genius of poets of old lands, terrible in beauty, age, and power" to be ever-enduring bards. I am certain that as he sang of "Life immense in passion, pulse, and power," he too, no less than Whitman, was singing the Modern Man.

Šopov defined himself as a reader of the ashes, not a reader of the stars. The stars are unattainable, while ashes are everywhere around us. The stars are silent, which is why they have so much power over us, while the ashes are themselves silence—one that tells all kinds of stories about humanity. It seems to me that my father seized the silence of both so he could bury in it all that remains unsaid, and it is in the unsaid that the poetic charge of his work resides. I have noted, for example, that, until the last years of his life, my father nowhere in his poetry mentioned by name either his mother or his homeland, but, in my opinion, they are two of the few defining words in his work.

For decades, whenever I have been asked to write something about my father, what catches in my throat are not words, but gnarls, as in his poem "Birth of the Word." For me, he became "that thing that weighed on me and pained me" (to quote his poem "In Silence"), something no words can express.

About thirty years ago, for a similar volume of his poetry published in France, I wrote a short text about my father, a portrait from which I can neither separate nor free myself. That was ten years after his death. Today, more than forty years have passed since he died and it is now time for a large collection of his poetry to appear in English, in the United States. I offer you, in the paragraphs below, this same portrait as my gift, at the entrance to this book of which my father would say (if he did not bury in silence the most essential words): "This is my legacy."

In 1982, my father's life burned out. The poems remain. Although they do not give a complete picture of their author—a handsome man, somewhat taciturn and discreet, but no less companionable; of slender, almost delicate stature; with green eyes of profound tenderness, sheltered by thick eyebrows—the poems nevertheless express the most essential thing: the intensity of being. Embodied in the images particular to my father's poetry, this intensity takes the form of flame, fire, sun, a magnificent conflagration, at once destructive and creative, which, after it reduced everything to ruin and rubble, rises from the ashes, following the dictate of some primordial curse, and gives birth to the new day.

For some forty years my father's infinite silence has burned within me, and day after day, in his stead, it tells me his great phoenix dream. Bringing these poems into English—which foretell in the ashes the signs of our own not-being—was the only way for me to share his dream . . . to converse with the silence.

The Fire Is Here:
The Long Journey of Aco Šopov

Rawley Grau and Christina E. Kramer

In the poem "An Event by the Lake" ["Nastan na ezerskiot breg"], Aco Šopov tells the story of a winged horse that, after traveling the world, returns exhausted to his native lake to be restored by its "clear and health-giving water." The people watching him question whether there was any point to his journey, but for the horse, we are told, it was "the highest purpose of his life: to discover his native land by discovering the world." At the end of the poem, the horse regains his strength by diving into the lake and flies off again, "carrying with him his highest purpose: to discover his native land and so discover the world."

Šopov wrote this poem in the early 1970s, when he was already one of the most celebrated poets in his native Macedonia, then part of Yugoslavia. At the time he was serving as the Yugoslav ambassador to Senegal, and, although he had made trips to several European cities, this was the first time he had lived for an extended period in a place so different from his own country, so the reciprocal discovery he talks about—to find one's homeland in the world and the world in one's homeland—is all the more striking. While it bears witness to the poet's deep connection with all of humanity, regardless of continent, race, climate, or history, it also seems an apt metaphor for Šopov's own poetic mission: to develop a poetry rooted in his own ancient culture and language that is simultaneously universal and modern, and to do this not by turning away from tradition but by drawing on something at the core of both the traditional and the modern, some truth that is both of the moment and beyond the realm of time.

Aco Šopov came of age with Macedonian poetry and was at the heart of its maturation into a modern literature. Although the Macedonian people enjoy a long, primarily oral, poetic tradition, their literary tradition is relatively new. Macedonia itself was not established as an official political entity until August 1944, when it became a constitutive republic within the newly declared federal state of Yugoslavia (on territory that was still being liberated from the Axis Powers). It was only then that the Macedonian language was finally standardized and made the official language of the Socialist Republic of Macedonia. The language's codification and new official status ensured a revitalized environment for creative expression, particularly in poetry. As the literary scholar Milne Holton noted: "This liberation of a language and a poetry was, of course, the culmination of a long historical process which has generated not only a language and a literature but a national consciousness and a special imagination peculiar to a people whose sad past has long been submerged in events of greater moment."[1]

While earlier poets such as the brothers Konstantin and Dimitar Miladinov, Grigor Prličev, and, especially, Kočo Racin had laid the groundwork for a new literary verse, modern Macedonian poetry came into its own only after World War II with Blaže Koneski, Slavko Janevski, and Aco Šopov, all of whom also made substantial contributions to the development of the scholarly, educational, and cultural institutions necessary for an educated, literate society. Šopov's role in this process was well described in 1970 by the critic Draško Ređep in his review of the book *Reader of the Ashes* [*Gledač vo pepelta*]: "This is, above all, an author who, over the past quarter-century of Macedonian poetry's life and growth, has been in many respects its synonym—its representative and, in many ways, its most influential part."[2]

·

1. Milne Holton, "Beyond Affirmation: Macedonian Poetry Since World War II," *Southeastern Europe/L'Europe du sud-est* 9 (1982): 161.
2. Draško Ређep, "Crno sunce Aca Šopova," *Izraz* (Sarajevo) 14, no. 11, p. 504.

Aco Šopov was born on December 20, 1923, in the city of Štip, in the eastern part of what is now the independent Republic of North Macedonia, but at the time was a region within the Kingdom of the Serbs, Croats, and Slovenes, later called Yugoslavia. The country into which he was born had been founded just five years earlier after decades of upheaval that included the end of the five-hundred-year reign of the Ottoman Empire, two Balkan Wars fought by Greece, Serbia, Bulgaria, and Montenegro over the Macedonian territories, the partition of those territories in 1913, and World War I. At the time of Šopov's birth, his native land was known as South Serbia, a name it would carry until the Axis invasion of Yugoslavia in 1941 and its occupation by Bulgaria.

Šopov's childhood was marked not only by the general poverty and turmoil in the region, but also by family difficulties, in particular the frequent absence of his psychologically troubled father, Ǵorǵi Zafirov-Šopov, and the long, paralyzing illness of his mother, Kostadinka Ruševa, a schoolteacher who instilled in him a love of poetry. Aco was the middle of three sons, of whom the older had been sent to study at the Eastern Orthodox seminary in Prizren, about a hundred miles away. When their mother became paralyzed in 1934, it was left to ten-year-old Aco to care for both her and his younger brother. The poet would later refer to this period in his life as a "hundred-headed monster." Nevertheless, all three brothers were educated. Aco completed secondary school in Štip, where he became interested in the socialist movement. He had begun writing poetry at the age of fourteen—mournful personal verses—but now he turned to social themes and, with two other students, published the underground Macedonian-language newspaper *The Spark* [*Iskra*].

In 1940, while still in secondary school, Šopov joined the League of Communist Youth of Yugoslavia. The following year, in early April, Germany invaded Yugoslavia, which quickly surrendered and was divided up, with most of Macedonia annexed to Bulgaria, an ally of Nazi Germany and Fascist Italy. Šopov's mother died in 1942, and in fall 1943 he joined the antifascist Macedonian armed resistance, fighting to liberate Macedonia from the Bulgarian occupation. These fighters were part of the broader Yugoslav Partisan movement that had been founded by the Yugoslav Communist leader, Josip Broz Tito, soon after the invasion. Šopov continued writing poetry as a Partisan combatant and served as literary editor of and contributor to *Fire* [*Ogin*], the newspaper of the Third Macedonian Shock Brigade. In fall 1944 his first poetry collection, *Poems* [*Pesni*], was printed by the underground press. It was the first Macedonian book to be published on liberated territory.

In the years following the war, Šopov published three books—*Railway of Youth* [*Pruga na mladost*] (1946) with the poet Slavko Janevski and *On Gramos* [*Na Gramos*] and *With Our Hands* [*So naši race*] (both in 1950)—works marked largely by reflections on the socialist revolution and national liberation. The poem "Eyes" ["Oči"], first published in 1946 and later included in *With Our Hands*, was dedicated to Šopov's Partisan comrade and first love Vera Jociḱ, who died after being wounded in battle. It remains one of Šopov's best-loved works, and the poet himself, in a 1966 interview, called it one of his favorite poems.[3]

In 1948, Marshal Tito broke with Stalin, which led to Yugoslavia's expulsion from the Communist Information Bureau. Among other momentous changes, this break signaled the beginning of the end of Soviet-style socialist realism as the only permitted doctrine in the arts. In October 1952, at the Third Congress of Yugoslav Writers, the Croatian writer Miroslav Krleža gave a famous speech calling for an end to socialist realism and stressing the need for creative freedom, and a month later the Yugoslav Communist leadership confirmed this new direction at the party congress in Zagreb. Writers, artists, publishers, and others were now allowed much greater freedom to make their own decisions about themes and styles, a move that opened the way to the modernist tendencies that would dominate Yugoslav culture well into the 1980s.

Šopov himself had been criticized for diverging from socialist realism at least since 1950, when he began publishing highly personal poems stemming from the breakup of his first marriage (to Blagorodna Cvetkovska) and his separation from his son, Vladimir, who was born in 1948. These poems were

---

3. Aco Šopov, "'Oči'—mojata najdobra pesna," interviewed by Stalin Lozanovski, *Mlad borec*, November 11, 1966, p. 15. For more on the importance of this poem, see the notes at the end of this book.

collected as *Verses of Suffering and Joy* [*Stihovi na makata i radosta*] in 1952, a month before Krleža's speech, and the turn from social topics to intimate themes sparked controversy in the Macedonian press. Šopov continued to develop this personal lyricism in his next two books, *Merge with the Silence* [*Slej se so tišinata*] (1955) and *The Wind Carries Beautiful Weather* [*Vetrot nosi ubavo vreme*] (1957), both of which won Macedonia's Kočo Racin Prize for poetry. As the literary scholar Graham W. Reid noted, this period marked "a turning point in Šopov's poetry and conceivably in Macedonian poetry at large." "Consistently writing out of individual experience," Reid continues, "Šopov now began to address his readers as individuals rather than as collectivized humankind."[4] *Merge with the Silence* and *The Wind Carries Beautiful Weather* are notable, too, for poems in which Šopov thematizes his destiny as a poet, such as "I Seek My Own Voice" ["Go baram svojot glas"] and "At the Lake" ["Na ezero"] in the former collection and "The White Sorrow of the Spring" ["Bela taga na izvorot"] and "Call Me Sky" ["Kaži mi nebo"] in the latter. Also striking is his use of the lyric miniature—jewel-like poems of no more than eight lines.

Not-Being [*Nebidnina*] appeared in 1963. This was another deeply personal collection, in which many of the poems were inspired by his love for Svetlana Velkovska, whom he married in 1958. The book is about much more than love for a woman, however. As the title suggests, the personal expands into a broader, more philosophical dimension,[5] in which healing love is related to something mysterious that transcends existence and lies at the very root of poetry. *Not-Being* opens with one of Šopov's key poems, "Birth of the Word" ["Raǵanje na zborot"], which serves as a prologue to the cycle "Prayers of My Body" ["Molitvi na moeto telo"]. Written in an intensely focused, meditative tone of pain, love, and hope sustained over eleven poems, the cycle is an achievement worthy to stand among the great works of postwar European poetry.

---

4. Graham W. Reid, "Aco Šopov," *South Slavic Writers Since World War II*, ed. Vasa D. Mihailovich, *Dictionary of Literary Biography*, vol. 181 (Detroit: Gale Research, 1997), p. 338.

5. In this connection, it may be worth noting that in 1961 Šopov graduated from the University of Skopje with a degree in philosophy.

On the morning of July 26, 1963—the same year that *Not-Being* was published—the city of Skopje, Macedonia's capital, was struck by a devastating earthquake. Over a thousand people were killed, several thousand were injured, and over a hundred thousand were left homeless. Šopov responded to the disaster with some of his most powerful poems, including "Horrordeath" ["Grozomor"], "August" ["Avgust"], and "Lament from the Other Side of Life" ["Tažačka od onaa strana na životot"]. These works first appeared in 1964 and 1965 in the literary journal *Modernity* [*Sovremenost*], with which Šopov was closely connected, and then in three collections of selected poems published later in the decade. The poet's most immediate literary response, however, was the prose piece "At Five Seventeen" ["Vo pet i sedumnaeset"], published in both the Macedonian and Serbian press soon after the earthquake occurred. Given the text's importance, we offer a translation of it as an appendix to this volume.

In 1970, Šopov published *Reader of the Ashes* [*Gledač vo pepelta*], which consisted entirely of poems written since *Not-Being*, including those inspired by the earthquake. More than just a collection of new poems, this is a clearly structured work with themes, images, and symbols echoing from poem to poem to create an energy and rhythm that draw the reader into its drama of suffering, love, and emergent meaning. Opening with the cycle "The Long Coming of the Fire" ["Dolgo doaǵanje na ognot"], it moves to eight more loosely connected poems of cataclysm and self-examination, which are grouped under the heading "Reader of the Ashes." This is followed by two more cycles, each of three poems: "Black Horsemen, White Riders" ["Crni konjanici, beli konjici"] and the apocalyptic "Black Sun" ["Crno sonce"]. Although many of the poems in this book can be read individually as reflecting the poet's personal struggles, when taken together they build into something much more expansive. "The fire is here, beneath these mad waters," Šopov declares in the opening line of the poem "The Long Coming of the Fire," restating this a few verses later as "The fire is here, underneath this hide" and commanding us (and himself): "Dig, / dig it up." The desire to reach some primordial creative/destructive force that is also deep within us—already present in

Not-Being—now in *Reader of the Ashes* acquires new urgency and complexity. At the same time, the journey he expresses in both books is implicitly entwined with the turbulent history and destiny of his homeland.

By the early 1970s, Šopov was a towering figure on the literary scene. He had won several important awards for his work, including, in 1970, Yugoslavia's highest honor in culture and science, the AVNOJ Award. That same year, he received his third Kočo Racin Prize, for *Reader of the Ashes*. As early as 1947 he had been one of the eight founding members of the Macedonian Writers' Association, and in 1951 he started the Kočo Racin Publishing House (named, like the award, for the poet, who died at the age of thirty-four as a Partisan fighter), which was later renamed Makedonska kniga [Macedonian Book]. Šopov also led the initiative to create, in the town of Struga on Lake Ohrid, the Struga Poetry Evenings, an internationally important annual poetry festival that today is considered to be the oldest continuous event of its kind in the world. In 1967 he was named one of the first members of the Macedonian Academy of Sciences and Arts and the following year was elected as a corresponding member of the Serbian Academy. It is also worth mentioning that in the mid-1960s, in a departure from his usual poetic practice, Šopov published a series of poems satirizing various aspects of contemporary Yugoslav society, which he collected in 1968 under the title *Jus-univerzum* (a possible translation might be *The YUniverse*), Macedonia's first book of satirical verse.

Šopov was appointed as the Yugoslav ambassador to Senegal in 1971, a decision that is not as surprising as it might seem at first. The president of Senegal was the renowned poet Léopold Sédar Senghor, one of the founders of the Négritude movement, and the country was a member of the Non-Aligned Movement, which Yugoslavia had co-founded and on which its position in world affairs significantly depended. As ambassador, Šopov was tasked with persuading Senghor to become more involved in the Non-Aligned Movement and to encourage other West African nations to do the same. The Belgrade authorities were undoubtedly counting on the two men to find a mutual language in diplomacy as much as in poetry. Šopov's diplomatic mission was capped off by Senghor's official visit to Yugoslavia, where the Senegalese president was received by Tito at the latter's state villa on Lake Bled, in Slovenia, and then traveled to Lake Ohrid to receive the Struga festival's highest award, the Golden Wreath.

Šopov's years in Africa, from 1971 to 1975, had a substantial impact on his writing. Senghor's influence can be seen in, among other things, the long discursive lines in a number of the poems from this period. On a more personal level, the poet experienced a genuine connection with the peoples and cultures of West Africa. To some extent, this may have been due to Macedonia's own centuries-long history of oppression under foreign powers, but for Šopov it went deeper than that. In the poem "Into the Black Woman's Dream" ["Vo sonot na crnata žena"], he addresses "the Black woman"—a symbol of Africa itself—as "a dark light that leads me down a narrow, dangerous path, / haunting me since childhood, / since before my childhood, from my mother's womb, / from my first, my most unconscious beginnings." In his African poems, Šopov's pursuit of that creative/destructive impulse, which he expressed so powerfully in *Reader of the Ashes* and *Not-Being*, gains new dimensions through his reflection on the commonality of human experience and his effort to understand and identify with the traumatic history of the Atlantic slave trade. It is in this context of trauma and revelation that Šopov articulates the idea, in "An Event by the Lake," that the discovery of the world and the discovery of one's native land are inextricably connected. Upon his return to Macedonia, Šopov published *The Song of the Black Woman* [*Pesna na crnata žena*, 1976], for which he received the Miladinov Brothers Award at the Struga poetry festival.

A year earlier, in 1975, he had published his translation of a large selection of Senghor's poetry, which, in a way, we can view as part of Šopov's effort to bring his discovery of the world to his homeland. Translation, indeed, was something Šopov was involved with throughout his career. In the 1950s, he had focused on translating poems for children, such as Ivan Krylov's fables (from Russian), Charles Perrault's fairy tales (from French), and Oton Župančič's collection of children's verse *Ciciban* (from Slovenian). Other translations included Eduard Bagritsky's *Lay of Opanas* (from Russian, with Slavko Janevski) and Edmond Rostand's *Cyrano de Bergerac* and Pierre Corneille's *Le Cid* (from French), as well as, from Serbo-Croatian, poets such as Jovan Jovanović Zmaj, Grigor Vitez, Miroslav Krleža, Izet Sarajlić, and Dragutin Tadijanović. Most notably, he translated Shakespeare's *Hamlet* in 1960, for which he won Macedonia's most important cultural honor, the October 11th Award, as well as a collection of Shakespeare's sonnets, which appeared in 1968.[6]

In 1976, Šopov was appointed as the president of Macedonia's Commission for Foreign Cultural Relations. The following year, however, his declining health forced him to retire from public life. Over the next few years, he sought treatment in hospitals in Ljubljana, Paris, Zagreb, and Moscow for a disease of the blood vessels that was progressively affecting his ability to walk and speak. He continued to write poetry nevertheless, much of it dealing with his illness. In these poems, which he published in 1980 under the title *The Tree on the Hill* [*Drvo na ridot*], we find many echoes from earlier work: the fire in the breast, the spreading blood, the plunging into waves, the lonely tree. Here, too, in a number of poems, he speaks more explicitly than ever before about his love for Macedonia and his childhood in Štip.[7] Despite its themes of illness and impending death, *The Tree on the Hill* is suffused with light, love, and transcendence.

In 1981, Šopov published his last book, *Scar* [*Luzna*], which brought together a large number of poems from across his lyric books since *Merge with the Silence*, along with his beloved poem "Eyes." Šopov made the selection himself, with the intention that this book would represent his poetic legacy. That same year he received Macedonia's October 11th Award for Lifetime Achievement. He died on April 20, 1982, at the age of fifty-eight, leaving behind his wife, Svetlana, and two children, Vladimir and Jasmina.

•

During the poet's lifetime, collections of his poems appeared in several languages, including Hungarian, Russian, French, and Romanian. Posthumous books were published in Spanish (1987, Mexico) and French

---

6. For his translation of *Hamlet*, Šopov relied on the Russian translation of the play by the poet Boris Pasternak, as he explained in a note to the book.

7. Unfortunately, we were not able to include these poems in our selection.

(1994). More recently, Šopov's poetry has appeared in a new Spanish translation (2011, Argentina), as well as in German (2012, Luxembourg). This year, to mark the one hundredth anniversary of his birth, collections have been published in Polish and Arabic (Tunisia). This book, also set to mark the poet's centennial, is the first significant collection of his poems to appear in English.[8]

All three centennial translations, as well as several others before, were initiated by Jasmina Šopova, the poet's daughter. In our case, Jasmina wrote to Christina in the fall of 2020, asking if she would be interested in translating a selection of her father's poems. Christina, thinking it would be good to have someone working on the project with more experience in poetry translation, suggested her friend Rawley. Jasmina saw that the combination of Rawley's experience as a translator of Russian and Slovenian poetry and Christina's deep knowledge of Macedonia's language and culture could form the basis of a vibrant collaboration that drew on the linguistic and literary skills and knowledge of both. Jasmina herself, whose knowledge of Aco Šopov's poetry is unsurpassed, was the third member of our team. It was she who chose the poems to be translated—a selection based largely on *Scar*—although we also offered a few suggestions in this regard. She carefully read every translation we made, providing valuable insights, comments, and, where necessary, corrections, for which we are immensely grateful.

Neither translator had much experience with collaborative translation, nor had we read Šopov. Rawley, with Christina's help, was just beginning to learn Macedonian. So we began tentatively, taking our first steps "in a kind of fog that is both frightening and exciting," as Jasmina put it in an early email, but we soon developed a good working process. Christina, in Toronto, would send Rawley, in Slovenia, the poem in three versions: the original Macedonian with marked stresses; an interlinear translation noting

---

8. The only previous collection of Šopov's work in English is a small-edition publication titled *The Word's Nativity* (2011), which was produced in haste as part of a massive but poorly conceived translation project by the Macedonian government under Nikola Gruevski. The translations, which show the main translator's unfamiliarity with contemporary literary English, are marred by numerous mistakes and unfortunate lexical choices.

linguistic details about particular words and significant cultural references; and a first, more or less literal, translation. From this material, Rawley created a draft that sought to capture the poetry of the original (rhythm, rhyme scheme, imagery) while preserving its meaning. Drafts went back and forth with questions and comments as we revisited our decisions, often with input from native speakers, until we eventually settled on a near-final version, which we then sent to Jasmina. As we became more familiar with Šopov's work, noticing especially his development of images and ideas across books and over decades, we revised our earlier translations to bring such connections to the fore. Meeting on Zoom, we read entire cycles out loud, alternating between the original and the translation. We came to realize that Šopov had created a remarkably coherent conceptual system—a poetic universe—and that it was essential to convey this in our translations.

A salient example was our handling of the Macedonian word *pesna*, which can refer either to a song or a poem. It is a key word for Šopov, who at times even addresses it directly, as in "Reader of the Ashes," one of the first poems we translated. That poem opens with the words "*Izgasni pesno . . .* " ["Burn out, *pesna* . . . "]. Since it seemed likely that the poet could be addressing the poem he was writing, or hoped to write, we initially translated this as "Burn out, poem . . . " But much later, when we were working on the cycles in the book *Reader of the Ashes*, it became clear that Šopov's notion of *pesna* transcended any individual poem or even the idea of a poem. It was instead connected with something from the beginning of time and also seemed to relate to both the folk-song tradition of Macedonia (the "song of old" in "The White Sorrow of the Spring") and the mysterious female figure who appears in *Not-Being*. In the poem "Black Sun," for example, the speaker exclaims: "O *pesna*, land, woman, O life and death at once, / whatever you bring me today, I will thirstily drink up." With this in mind, we reviewed our earlier translations and, in most cases, changed "poem" to "song."

As we became more aware of such interconnections, we realized that to preserve the integrity of the poet's vision, the poems had to be read in groups—ideally, in the same groups the poet had used when organizing his books. We were particularly struck by the power of the collection

Reader of the Ashes and knew that we wanted to present this masterwork as a whole. The same was true when we reexamined Šopov's previous book, *Not-Being*. Consequently, when it came to structuring our own book, we decided that it should open with these two impressive works from the prime of his career, followed by the most important poems from earlier collections and ending with representative selections from his last two books, *The Song of the Black Woman* and *The Tree on the Hill*. We were reluctant, however, to start the book right off with the Prayer Cycle (as *Not-Being* does) and so decided to follow what Šopov did when he was organizing *Scar*, using the same two poems—"Down Below There Is a Blood" and "Scar"—to lead the reader into Šopov's poetic world. We should also note that, while Šopov generally did not revise his poems once they had been published in a book, in cases where variations do exist, we take the *Scar* version as the basis for our translation.

Unlike the usual single-translator process, where decisions are largely intuitive, our back-and-forth dialogue forced us to articulate the reasons behind our choices. We thus alerted each other to possible overinterpretations that departed from the poet's actual meaning or, on the contrary, overly precise renderings that failed to capture the spirit of the line. We learned to be content with ambiguity. Šopov often blurs the boundaries between subject and object, between the one who acts and the one who is acted upon. In "Second Prayer of My Body" ["Vtora molitva na moeto telo"], for example, it is not clear if the bridge wants to see itself in the wave, or the wave wants to glimpse its face in the light it reflects onto the bridge. Our translation, then, while always striving for precision, also had to allow for openness. To borrow an image from "August," Šopov's poems create nets of meaning in which golden fish are dreaming, and as translators we had to capture not just the cords of the net but also the spaces between them.

Translating poetry is particularly challenging because you are working in a small space. While there might be several ways to resolve a dilemma when translating prose, with poetry the choices are narrowed by the constraints of the form—line length, the shape of the stanza, rhythm, rhyme, and other effects. From a linguistic perspective, differences between grammatical categories are drawn acutely in seemingly small variations. For example, both Macedonian and English have a category of definiteness—the contrast between saying *a* book and *the* book parallels the contrast in Macedonian between *kniga* and *knigata*. Macedonian also developed an optional, although by no means regular, indefinite article from the number one, *edna*, that does not always correspond to the English article *a/an*—the Macedonian word generally points to something specific but not definite: a certain book. Translating such distinctions can be tricky, especially when the poet himself steps outside of conventional usage. An example is the title of "Down Below There Is a Blood," which translates the Macedonian "Dolu ima *edna* krv." Using the indefinite article with the mass noun "blood" sounds a bit strange, and, in fact, in earlier drafts we decided against it. But Šopov's use of *edna* is also odd here, and we made it a general rule to "trust the poet." Our final version of the title seeks to capture the strangeness and strength of the original.

Another parallel is that Macedonian, like English, has lost the use of most grammatical cases, i.e. changes in nouns and adjectives that indicate a word's semantic relation to other words in the same sentence. Instead, it relies heavily on prepositions, some of which can express various relationships. The preposition *na*, for instance, may indicate possession ("of"), location ("at"), or the indirect object ("to"). More than once we debated the meaning of this preposition and on several occasions asked native speakers to tell us how they understood a certain phrase. The line in "August" about nets offers a good illustration of such dilemmas. In Macedonian, it reads: "Ribarite na tvojot pogled pletat nevidlivi mreži," which could be rendered, more or less word-for-word, as "The fishermen in/of your gaze weave invisible nets." One of our early drafts interpreted the phrase *na tvojot pogled* as "in your view/sight," suggesting that the fishermen are seen by the speaker (who is speaking to himself here). But then we wondered if *na* could indicate possession: "the fishermen *of* your gaze"—as if they were somehow weaving their nets inside the eyes. Our final draft became: "The fishermen in your eyes weave nets unseen," a wording that allows for both readings and captures the kind of subject/object ambiguity typical of Šopov: are the fishermen seen by the gaze or are they themselves the vehicles of sight?

Other challenges related to Šopov's choice of specific words. We spent days discussing how to translate the names of certain plants mentioned in the poems,[9] and sometimes the names of the poems themselves. In the case of "Horrordeath," the solution was relatively easy: the Macedonian title, "Grozomor," is a compound the poet coined from the word *groza*, meaning "horror," and the Slavic stem *-mor-*, which relates to large-scale death and destruction. Rather than use an ordinary English word such as "horror," we devised our own compound.

There are, indeed, a fair number of coined words in these poems, and we did our best to reflect them in our translation. But Šopov's most famous coinage, a word that feels more like a discovery than an invention, is *nebidnina*, which he first used in 1963 as the title for a complex poem about the journey from loneliness and pain to love and healing, and then as the title of the book in which the poem appeared. Although on the surface, the word might seem easy enough to translate, it presented one of our greatest challenges. It is a noun derived from the verb *bide*, "to be," with the negating prefix *ne*. So perhaps *nonbeing, nonexistence,* or *unbeing*. But it is clear from the poems in which it appears that it refers to something more than nonexistence or simple nothingness. Šopov himself, in various interviews, discussed the difficulty of defining the word. As he was preparing the book for publication, he noted that the title "could mean, roughly, something that is impossible, something that will not be realized" and that he was using it to underscore the paradox that "poetry, however much we might understand it and create it as something essential, as something more than what we usually understand by the concept 'life'... is still, even in its most perfect form and highest achievements, incapable of grasping all the richness and complexity of this concept."[10] Many years later, in a magazine interview, he explained: "*Nebidnina* I understand as realization through nonrealization. I did not reach this awareness suddenly or consciously; rather, it is a result of my poetic experience to which I come closer with

---

9. See, for example, our comments on "elderwort" (in "Scar") and "snake-berry" (in "Horrordeath") in the notes on those poems.

10. From an interview on the program *Panorama*, Radio-Television Skopje, January 16, 1962.

every poem."[11] Given the elusiveness that the poet himself attached to the term, we wanted a word that could be as open as possible and hold various meanings of nonexistence, nonbeing, and unbeing, while also suggesting something new, something unattainable yet always potent in its absence, and so we chose the unusual hyphenated word *not-being*.

Šopov employs a wide range of poetic forms in his work: from the miniatures of the 1950s collections to the intricate four- and five-line rhymed stanzas that characterize the Prayer Cycle (and many other poems as well) to the couplets in the cycles of *Reader of the Ashes* and the long discursive lines of his later poetry. The vast majority of his poems use rhyme, often with a very clear rhyme scheme, but even when he ventures closer to free verse, repetition and rhythm remain defining elements. In a 1965 interview, he stated: "I strive for a kind of formal perfection and want this formal perfection to also be justified internally by the content."[12] Šopov's meter tends to be irregular, composed of two-beat and three-beat measures in different combinations with lines of varying length. But the rhythm is almost always distinct, at times even pounding (as in the Fire Cycle). In our translations we sought to preserve as much as possible the form and energy of the originals, without, however, resorting to anything contrived or strained. We used rhyme where we could, but we were often content to merely suggest the idea of rhyme through some phonetic or visual correspondence.

Šopov was fully aware of his responsibility as a modern Macedonian poet, crafting richly textured, complex poems in a once-suppressed language for a people whose national identity had itself only recently been officially recognized. Something of this is expressed in the poem "If There Isn't Enough Light for You" ["Ako ti nedostasuva svetlina"]. Read alone, it sounds like a touching love poem, a lover's promise to do all he can to comfort and console his beloved. But when we read it in the context in which it appears in *Reader of the Ashes*, coming immediately after the "Lament

---

11. "Aco Šopov pred dvanaeset prašalnici," *Razvitok* 17, no. 2, March–April 1979.

12. "Aco Šopov, pesnik za koga je vezana evolucija makedonskog poetskog izraza," *Duga*, interviewed by Predrag Protić, March 25, 1965.

from the Other Side of Life" and surrounded by other poems written in response to the devastation of the Skopje earthquake, we hear the poet expressing his love to his grieving nation, promising to use all his abilities to assuage their unfathomable sorrow.

The love is reciprocal. Many Macedonians can still recite verses learned in school from the Partisan poem "Eyes" and they are familiar with the story of the heroic woman it celebrates. The four-line poem "In Silence" ["Vo tišina"], which joins form and content near perfectly, is similarly widely known and cherished. The word *nebidnina* has become part of the language, although most Macedonians would be hard-pressed to define it. While it is impossible for us, as translators, to fully mediate the experience of Šopov's Macedonian readers, the notes at the back of the book seek to clarify a few of the more important cultural references in the poems. We also try to provide other useful information that will deepen the reader's experience of Šopov's poetry.

Taken as a whole, one might be tempted to view Šopov's work as a trajectory of self-exploration. A poem from the 1950s is titled, with charming obviousness, "I Seek My Voice," and twenty years later, as he visits the House of Slaves in Senegal, he declares: "here my primordial passion has summoned me / to discover my archetype" ("The Light of the Slaves"). But such an assessment misses the mark. With Šopov, we are not dealing with confessional or solipsistic poetry, although in places it may seem that way; ultimately, there is no self-obsession here. Rather, a focus on the self leads to what is universally human; the personal becomes primordial as the poet searches for the ordinary word not yet found, as he digs for the fire beneath the hide and the blood down below. This is a search full of paradox, rooted in his homeland but sought in the world, and vice versa. It pulsates with urgency, yet demands patience and struggle, for the fire is long in coming.

We are honored to be able to present the poems of this modernist master to the English-speaking world, and we can only hope that something of Šopov's fire burns in these translations.

Acknowledgments

Every translation requires editors, native speakers, colleagues, and friends who are willing to read and comment on drafts. In our work on Šopov's poetry we have been fortunate to have the help of a golden circle of people. First and foremost, we thank Jasmina Šopova for her confidence in us, her careful and critical reading of our translations, and for turning our Covid lockdowns into a moving experience of collaborative translation. We also wish to acknowledge the Aco Šopov Poetry Foundation and the extraordinary website they provide (www.acosopov.com), which Jasmina manages—this gave us access to all of Aco Šopov's poems, and in many cases their translations into other languages; his prose texts, articles, and interviews (including those cited in the introduction and in the notes on the poems); scholarly essays related to the poet; and other media as well, including video and audio recordings. We are also grateful to the editors Shook (of Phoneme Media) and Will Evans (of Deep Vellum), who recognized the unique opportunity to publish this book for the poet's centennial; we are indebted to their enthusiasm for Šopov's work and their commitment to creating this beautiful edition. We also thank the great team at Deep Vellum, who made this book a physical reality, in particular, Linda Stack-Nelson for her expert editing and management of production, Kirkby Gann Tittle for his beautiful typesetting and diligence with the Macedonian fonts, Chad Felix for his splendid cover design, and Sara Balabanlilar for overseeing the design process. We are deeply grateful to our Macedonian colleagues for their willingness to help with difficult vocabulary and unusual syntax, with special thanks going to Eleni Bužarovska, Liljana Mitkovska, Elena Petroska, Goce Smilevski, and others. The 2021 Summer School on Lake Ohrid, organized by the International

Seminar in Macedonian Language, Literature, and Culture, SS. Cyril and Methodius University, played an instrumental role in Rawley's progress with the language. Mary-Allen Johnson, Associate Professor and Curator of the Hilandar Research Library at Ohio State University, provided us with PDF copies of Šopov poetry collections that Christina had previously donated to the Library. We also thank Nova Generation, the United Macedonian Diaspora (UMD), and the Department of Slavic Languages and Literatures at the University of Toronto for their contributions to the publication of this volume. We thank, too, the people close to us, our families and friends, who listened to and critiqued our translations, who understood the intensity of the work, and who supported us as we, too, tried to seize the fire: Richard Franz, David Kramer, Victor Friedman, Paul Clyne, Saško Radomin, Tim Grau, Dušan Šarotar, and Lukas Debeljak, to name but a few.

THE LONG COMING OF THE FIRE

НЕБИДНИНА (1963)

NOT-BEING (1963)

ИМА ДОЛУ ЕДНА КРВ

Има долу тешка една крв
од древноста чиниш останата.
Не се ни назира во врелите маглини на овој врв.
Лежи проколната како лузна врз раната.

Има долу една тешка крв. Има крв една.
Има една крв густа како црна смола.
Крв незаситна и исконски жедна.
Има една стара крв, црна и гола.

Лежи она и рие како крт.
Оди од праг до праг, рие низ свеста.
Непогрешно и неизбежно како смрт
ги исполнува сите празнини и места.

Има долу тешка една крв,
една крв што секогаш вели:
следи ме покорно, следи ме прв,
никогаш од мене не се дели.

Има долу една страшна крв,
пострашна и од заканата.
Има долу една таква тешка крв
од древноста чиниш останата.

DOWN BELOW THERE IS A BLOOD

Down below there is a heavy blood,
left over, you might think, from an age long gone.
Up here in the sultry mists it is invisible.
Like a scar it lies cursed on top of the wound.

Down below there is a heavy blood. A single blood.
A blood that is black as pitch and as thick.
An insatiable blood with a primal thirst.
There is an old blood below, naked and black.

It lies below and burrows like a mole.
Threshold to threshold, it burrows through the mind.
Unerring as death and as inescapable,
it seeps into every last space and void.

Down below there is a heavy blood,
a single blood repeating constantly:
Follow and obey me, follow me first,
never must you be divided from me.

Down below there is a terrible blood,
more terrible even than the threat.
Down below there is such a heavy blood
you might think it was left by an age long dead.

ЛУЗНА

Те оградив со девет градини, крви,
те затворив во девет грла,
што бараш уште, зошто ме прогонуваш, крви,
зошто закануваш со своето копито темно,
зошто незасито?

Те оградив со девет градини, девет грла,
смири се, крви, слегни во своите темнини
на чие дно твојот црвен вепар
одамна бара пештера за починка.
Слези во своите темнини, крви,

и не обѕирај се,

нема подобро место од ова што ќе те скроти,
од овие девет градини, девет градини
што живеат од твоето зеленило,
од овие девет грла, девет грла
што ја пеат пролетта на твоите песни.
Слези во своите темнини, крви,

и не вели ми:

Слушај како татни од далечина,
слушај како татнат сите кории,
идат коњи по пат од ѕвезди и месечина,
идат коњи, коњи, коњи, коњи дории,
идат коњи да ме прегазат,
идат, идат ќе ме прегазат.
Но јас ќе ги ритнам со копитото

SCAR

I encircled you, blood, with nine gardens,
I enclosed you in nine gorges, nine throats—
what else do you want, why do you keep after me?
Why threaten me, blood, with your dark hoof?
Why so insatiable?

I encircled you with nine gardens, nine gorges,
so calm yourself, blood, settle into your darkness,
at the bottom of which, for a long, long time,
your red boar has been seeking a cave to rest in.
Descend into your darkness, blood,

and do not look back.

There is no better place to tame you than this,
than these nine gardens, nine gardens that live
on your lush vegetation;
than these nine gorges, nine throats that sing
the springtime of your songs.
Descend into your darkness, blood,

and do not say to me:

Listen to the thunder in the distance,
listen to the roaring of the forests—
horses are coming on a road of stars and moonlight,
horses, horses, horses are coming,
bay horses are coming to trample me,
they're coming to trample me underfoot.
But I will kick them with my hoof,

ќе ги ритнам право сред чело,
да ме паметат, да ме прикажуваат
и лузната да им свети навечер,
во нивните ноќи без месечина,
во нивните денови без светлина,
на нивните патишта под бурјани.

Не вели ми, крви. Крви, смири се,
оградена со девет градини,
затворена со девет грла
како некој семоќен владател
на некоја непристапна тврдина.

I will kick them in the middle of their foreheads
so they remember me, so they speak of me,
and in the evening that scar will shine for them,
will shine in their nights without moonlight,
will shine in their days without sunlight,
will shine on their paths through the elderwort.

Say nothing, blood. Blood, calm yourself,
encircled by nine gardens,
enclosed by nine gorges,
like an all-powerful ruler
in some inaccessible fortress.

МОЛИТВИ НА МОЕТО ТЕЛО

PRAYERS OF MY BODY

РАЃАЊЕ НА ЗБОРОТ

Глужд на глужд.
Камен врз камен.
Камена шума
изземнина.
Глужд на глужд.
Камен врз камен,
од камен и ние обата.
Чади ноќта.
Зборот се двои од темнината.
Модар јаглен му гори во утробата.
О ти што постоиш зашто не постоиш
небото го лулаш,
земјата ја вртиш.
О ти што постоиш зашто не постоиш
земјата јачи под камени плочници.
Иде замелушен од своите смрти
зборот што ги крши сите слепоочници.
Глужд на глужд.
Камен врз камен.
Својот гроб со прокуда го копам.
Отвори ме
проклетио,
ти тврдино камена,
да изгорам во јагленот на зборот,
да се стопам.

BIRTH OF THE WORD

Gnarl upon gnarl.
Stone upon stone.
Stone forest
frozensolidness.
Gnarl upon gnarl.
Stone upon stone,
stone, too, the both of us.
Smoke rises in the night.
The word separates from the darkness,
blue coal burning in its bowels.
O you who exist because you do not exist,
you shake the sky
you spin the earth.
O you who exist because you do not exist,
the earth groans beneath stone plates.
Dazed from its dyings, the word comes forth—
the word that splinters all our temples.
Gnarl upon gnarl.
Stone upon stone.
Out of bad habit I dig my grave.
Open me,
accursed one,
you fortress of stone,
that I may burn in the coals of the word
and melt away.

МОЛИТВА ЗА ЕДЕН ОБИЧЕН НО УШТЕ НЕПРОНАЈДЕН ЗБОР

Телото мое те моли:
Пронајди збор што личи на обично дрво
што личи на дланки јагленосани и прародителски голи,
што е како чедност во секое молење прво.
За таков збор телото мое те моли.

Телото мое те моли:
Пронајди збор од кој — штом со крик ќе се рече —
несвесно крвта почнува да боли,
крвта што бара корито да тече.
За таков збор телото мое те моли.

Пронајди таков вистински збор
налик на сите мирни заробеници
на оној ветар, оној развигор
што ги буди срните во нашите зеници.
Пронајди таков вистински збор.

Пронајди збор на раѓање, на лелекање,
пронајди таков збор. И овој храм
затворен во својата древност и голем од чекање
ќе ти се отвори покорно и сам.
Пронајди збор на раѓање, на лелекање.

PRAYER FOR AN ORDINARY WORD NOT YET FOUND

My body beseeches you:
Find it a word that is like ordinary wood,
like hands that are charred and as bare as our ancestors,
like the innocence of all the first prayers ever prayed.
For such a word, my body beseeches you.

My body beseeches you:
Find it a word that—as soon as it's said as a cry—
the blood starts to ache without knowing why,
and looks for a channel in which it can flow.
For such a word, my body beseeches you.

Find it such a word, a word that is true,
that is like all the quiet captives held fast
by that soft wind, that southern breeze
which awakens the little deer in our eyes.
Find it such a word, a word that is true.

Find it a word of birth, of wailing,
find such a word. And this temple, locked
in its ancientness and large from waiting,
will open to you humbly, of its own accord.
Find it a word of birth, of wailing.

ВТОРА МОЛИТВА НА МОЕТО ТЕЛО

Ова тело што лежи како мост меѓу два брега,
ова тело што живее од мугрите на твоите желби,
ќе биде и утре како што е сега,
само со два белега повеќе од две лути стрелби,
ова тело што лежи како мост меѓу два брега.

Ова тело што лежи како мост и трпеливо одамна чека
да помине веселник некој и да го пробуди пак . . .
Протечи под ова тело како скротена река
да заечи силно од нежност со секој извиен лак
ова тело што лежи како мост и трпеливо одамна чека.

Ова тело што лежи како мост некој бран да го плени
за да го улови во него својот заборавен лик
ќе стане со сите будења и мени
на нестварни желби стварен светилник
ова тело што лежи како мост некој бран да го плени.

SECOND PRAYER OF MY BODY

This body which lies like a bridge between two shores,
this body which lives on the dawns of your desires,
will be even tomorrow the same as it is today,
but with two marks more from two sharp blasts of gunfire,
this body which lies like a bridge between two shores.

This body which lies like a bridge and waits long in patience
for someone jovial to come and wake it up again . . .
Flow beneath this body like a river that has been harnessed,
to echo strong in tenderness with every curving arch—
this body which lies like a bridge and waits long in patience.

This body which lies like a bridge, waiting for a wave to seize it,
to catch in it a glimpse of its own forgotten face,
will become through all these awakenings and phases
a tangible beacon of intangible desires,
this body which lies like a bridge, waiting for a wave to seize it.

ТРЕТА МОЛИТВА НА МОЕТО ТЕЛО

Што си: девојка, жена, мајка? Што си
ти што бдееш пред овој храм во кој со тишина се лечи
телото мое молитвено што клечи.
Светлина ли, мрак ли твоето идење му носи.
Што си: девојка, жена, мајка, што си?

Што си ти застаната со спокој темен
пред ова тело чиј глас со виј го гони
ветрот што лута под тајни небосклони,
чиј глас е жед и виј на вијот земен.
Што си ти застаната со спокој темен?

Што си ти: девојка, жена, мајка,
ти—скаменета пред влезот на овој храм
со моќно име: ПОБЕДУВАМ,
па ова тело возвишено го крена.
Што си ти: девојка, мајка, жена?

THIRD PRAYER OF MY BODY

What are you—girl, woman, mother? Which one
are you, keeping watch before this temple, where
silence heals my body, as it kneels in prayer.
What does your coming bring it—light or gloom?
What are you—girl, woman, mother? Which one?

What are you, standing so still in dark repose
in front of this body, whose voice with a cry pursues
the wind as it roves beneath secret skies,
whose voice is the thirst and cry of the earth's own cry?
What are you, standing so still in dark repose?

What are you? Are you girl, woman, mother?
You, still as stone before the door of this temple
bearing the mighty name I TRIUMPH—
you lifted this body up, exalted and solemn.
What are you? Are you girl, mother, woman?

ЧЕТВРТА МОЛИТВА НА МОЕТО ТЕЛО

Овде си, над ова тело, како смирено крило,
ти — толку разумно — толку студено штедра,
па сакам да се помолам за она што веќе било,
зашто иднината во сите срца е ведра.

Сплети ги тие светлини, тоа горење бело,
тие светкавици во темнина што спијат,
обви го со нив денес ова гордо исправено тело,
сеедно — како камшик или ко бршлан вијат.

Сплети ги во огромна лузна, скамени ги во вера,
дај ми, дај таа светлина со кошмар да ја пијам,
зашто сè она што потемнува во моето Вчера
јас како светло Утре во длабини го кријам.

FOURTH PRAYER OF MY BODY

You are here, above this body, like a restful wing,
you, who are so rationally, so coolly generous
that I want to plead for what has already been,
because the future in all hearts is cloudless.

Braid together those bright days, that white burning,
those flashes of lightning that sleep in darkness;
wrap them around this now proud, erect body,
as a whip or as ivy—it makes no difference.

Braid them in a giant scar, harden them into faith,
only give me, give me that light, to drink with nightmare,
because all that grows dark within my Yesterday
I hide in the depths as a radiant Tomorrow.

ПЕТТА МОЛИТВА НА МОЕТО ТЕЛО

Зар ќе го изодиш ова тело, овие шеметни височини
ветре на тишината, пеперуго на сонот недоболина.
Каде потаму во мене? Застани, неуморо, почини
на овој камен каракамен, на оваа голина.

Зар ќе испливаш од ова тело, од овој темен вител
танчарко на сите подземни, сите нескротени води.
Ти си само овде како прастар жител
и играш врз ова тело гневно што те роди.

Заробени сме сега во игра, во круг,
и носени од тмурна и нестварна плима
цел живот патуваме од еден до друг
и секој го крие она што го има.

FIFTH PRAYER OF MY BODY

So you will traverse this body, these vertiginous heights,
wind of silence, butterfly of a dream of everhurting.
Where next inside me? Stop, relentless one—rest
on this stone, this black stone, in this empty clearing.

So you will swim from this body, from this dark maelstrom,
dancer on all waters subterranean and unruly.
You are only here as an ancient dweller,
dancing across this body, which bore you in fury.

So now we are captive in a dance, in a circle;
we are carried on a dreary, unreal tidal wave,
and travel all our lives from one to the other,
each keeping hidden what it is we have.

ШЕСТА МОЛИТВА НА МОЕТО ТЕЛО

Везилка си на оваа игра, на овој домородски ритам.
Од дивина со крвта ми викаш, од далечина:
„Кон твоето тело неподвижно итам
јас непозната, глув водопад од месечина.

На твоето чело високо пасат плашливи елени,
ти имаш раце силни и зараснати длабоко вземи,
во твоето грло растат треви зелени,
твоите зборови се ковчести и остри, но неми.”

Везилка си на оваа игра, на овој домородска песна
а не знам дали си моја ноќ, дали си ден,
и оваа грутка црвеница врз која лежам е тесна
за овој пораз мој величествен.

SIXTH PRAYER OF MY BODY

You are the embroideress of this dance, this homeborn rhythm.
You call to me in my blood, from afar, from the wildland.
You say: "To your motionless body I hasten—
I, who am unknown, a muffled waterfall of moonlight.

High up on your forehead timid deer are grazing,
your hands are strong and joined deep in the earth,
growing in your throat are wild green grasses,
your words are bony and sharp, but they are mute."

You are the embroideress of this dance, this homeborn song,
but I do not know if you are my day or my night,
and narrow is the clump of red clay I lie upon,
too narrow for this, my magnificent defeat.

СЕДМА МОЛИТВА НА МОЕТО ТЕЛО

Твојата молбена закана, твојата лукавост нежна
и сите твои слатки измами ги знам.
Дали оваа игра денеска толку ми стежна
па пред тебе до болка и јас се разголувам.

Ти знаеш — на ова место нема никаква трага,
ни хишник овде ни ѕвер некаков мине.
Биди милозлива, биди дарежлива и блага
со ова тело од чекање што гине.

Ова тело личи на жедна суводолица
поцрнета од сонце, испукана од жега.
Ова тело е истрајно и гладно како јаловица.
Биди му родилка, зачни го повторно сега.

SEVENTH PRAYER OF MY BODY

Your entreatful menace, your tender cunning,
your sweet deceits—all these I know.
Does this dance today weigh so heavy upon me
that even I, till I ache, bare myself to you?

You know that there are no tracks in this place,
no predator is here, no wild beast passes by.
Be merciful, be generous and gentle with this body,
which in its waiting is wasting away.

This body is like a parched riverbed
cracked from the heat and blackened by sun.
This body is tenacious, hungry as a barren field.
Be its new mother, reconceive it now.

ОСМА МОЛИТВА НА МОЕТО ТЕЛО ИЛИ КОЈ ЌЕ ЈА СМИСЛИ ТАА ЉУБОВ

Под овој меч,
под овој меч на тишината,
под ова отворено небо,
овие трепетлики,
лежи ова в неврат издолжено тело,
со око стрела в око на вишините,
земјата ја корне со чело.
Под овој меч,
под овој меч на тишината
кој ќе ја смисли таа непозната љубов,
тој збор што не постои во речникот
на секиједневните средби,
на секидневните поздрави,
во очајот на оставените,
во мирот на погубените,
во гласот на вљубените.

Издолжено в неврат лежи ова тело,
со око стрела в око на вишините,
земјата ја корне со чело.
Земјо, ти веќе не си земја,
ти си грутка надеж,
црна од мака, од соништа зелена,
ти си око фрлено во вселена.
Кој ќе ја смисли таа непозната љубов —
пред ова будење
пред ова заспивање —
тоа чудо во чудо,
тоа завивање!

EIGHTH PRAYER OF MY BODY, OR,
WHO WILL CONCEIVE OF THAT LOVE?

Under this sword,
under this sword of silence,
under this open sky,
these quaking aspens,
stretched beyond return lies this body,
shooting an eye at the eye in the heavens,
harrowing the earth with its forehead.
Under this sword,
under this sword of silence,
who will conceive of that unknown love,
that word not found in the dictionary
of everyday encounters,
of everyday hellos,
in the despair of those left behind,
in the peace of those who have perished,
in the voice of those in love?

Stretched beyond return lies this body,
shooting an eye at the eye in the heavens,
harrowing the earth with its forehead.
Earth, no more are you earth;
you are a lump of hope,
black with pain, green with dreams;
you are an eye cast into the universe.
Who will conceive of that unknown love—
before this waking,
before this drifting into sleep—
that miracle in a miracle,
that howl?

Издолжено в неврат лежи ова тело
под овој меч,
под овој меч на тишината,
земјата ја корне со чело,
на рамо ја носи месечината.
Готово, месечино, довека готово!
Во твојата преполна шарена мрежа,
мрежа од страдања,
во твојата мрежа од лаги и измами
од притворства и слатки бладања,
од многу надежи изгубени,
нема веќе место за никого,
најмалку за тие што се вљубени.
Боли, месечино. Нека боли.
Болат твоите ребра погодени.
Под тебе светот и ние сме голи.
Штотуку родени.

Кој ќе ја смисли таа непозната љубов,
пред ова будење
пред ова заспивање. —
Тоа чудо во чудо,
тоа завивање.

Stretched beyond return lies this body,
under this sword,
under this sword of silence,
harrowing the earth with its forehead,
carrying the moon on its shoulder.
It's over, moon! Over forever!
In your colorful, overstuffed net,
your net of afflictions,
in your net of lies and deceits,
of dissemblances and sweet delusions,
of many lost hopes,
there is no room left for anyone,
least of all for those in love.
It hurts, moon. Let it hurt.
Your shattered ribs are painful.
Beneath you we and the world are naked.
Are just now born.

Who will conceive of that unknown love—
before this waking,
before this drifting into sleep—
that miracle in a miracle,
that howl?

ДЕВЕТТА МОЛИТВА НА МОЕТО ТЕЛО

Еве го тоа место, тоа неизодливо тело,
распослано како нема глад.
Еве ги сите светлини и води
на овој соѕидан град.

Врз кровот негов гука гулаб вечен —
чудна една сказна од леб и од сребро ...
Дали го откри тој збор, тоа име
што штрека во дното на секое ребро.

Дали ја откри таа страшна тајна,
тој уште нигде неживеан век,
дали откри колку светлините болат
над ова тело што тече без тек.

Еве го тоа место, тоа неизодливо тело,
таа глад што го распосла и роди.
Еве го овде тој соѕидан град,
соѕидан од светлини и води.

NINTH PRAYER OF MY BODY

This is that place, that untraversable body,
sprawling out like a voiceless hunger.
These are all the lights and the waters
of this city built within walls.

Up on the roof an eternal dove is cooing—
some marvelous tale of silver and bread . . .
Did you ever discover that word, that name,
which throbs in the marrow of every rib?

Did you ever discover that terrible secret,
that life which has nowhere yet been lived?
Did you ever discover how painful the lights are
above this body, which flows without flowing?

This is that place, that untraversable body,
that hunger which sprawled it out and gave it birth.
This is that city built here within walls,
within walls built of light and water.

ДЕСЕТТА МОЛИТВА НА МОЕТО ТЕЛО

Еве го тоа место, таа заробена убавина,
таа чудесна смрт од сино и бело,
од сино и бело во очите на ветрот,
еве го тој непрокопсаник, тоа тело.

Еве го тоа место, таа свенлива убавина,
пред сите сегашности и пред сите дамнини,
пред твоето исконско темно неспокојство —
тие неизодливи нерамнини.

Ти стоиш овде немо и притаено
над овој стивнат и непознат вител.
Биди му пролет жуберлива и лековита
ако би му била повелник и жител.

И без да прашаш со древна љубопитност
дали е верен пленик на вистините,
влези тивко и незабележано,
влези со мудроста на годините.

TENTH PRAYER OF MY BODY

This is that place, that captive beauty,
that miraculous death from blue and white,
from the blue and white in the eyes of the wind;
this is that brutish thing, that body.

This is that place, that beauty which pales
before all pasts and before all presents,
before your primordially dark unease—
this is that untraversable roughness.

You stand here silent and unseen
above this quieted, unknown maelstrom.
Be to it a burbling, health-giving springtime,
if you would command it and dwell within.

And without asking, anciently curious,
if it is a faithful prisoner of the verities,
enter quietly and unnoticed,
enter with the wisdom of the years.

ПОСЛЕДНА МОЛИТВА НА МОЕТО ТЕЛО

Црн е твојот ветар, а ноќта бела
и секој дамар напнат од зрелина.
Застани како меч во овој дрворед од тела
пред да се срушиш заслепено од белина.

Но и тогаш играта ќе продолжи пак
со иста таинственост и со иста чедност.
И тие треви што ќе те покријат со мрак
ќе изгорат во пожарот на твојата жедност.

LAST PRAYER OF MY BODY

Your wind is black and white is the night,
and every vein is swollen and ripe.
In this avenue of bodies, stand straight as a sword
before you collapse, blinded by white.

But the dance even then will continue as ever,
with the same mystery, with the same innocence.
And when those grasses cover you in darkness,
the blaze of your thirst will burn them away.

ПЕСНИТЕ И ГОДИНИТЕ

THE SONG AND THE YEARS

СТАРО КУПУВАМ

Старо купувам, старо купувам,
стари алишта, стари пискули,
старо железо, стари љубови,
старо купувам.
Купувам стари дребности,
непотребности,
чевли излижани, ризи износени,
среќи осреќени,
старо, старо, старо купувам.
Купувам стари секидневности,
мали и големи ревности,
стари елеци во долапите,
стари котли на огништата,
стари саѓи на совеста,
стара 'рѓа на соништата.
Старо, старо, старо купувам.
Купувам стари секидневности,
мали и големи ревности,
стари љубови, стари среќи, стари гревови,
купувам стари радости, стари младости,
старо, старо, старо купувам.

Старо купувам, старо купувам,
стари алишта, стари пискули,
старо железо, стари љубови.
Купувам стари секидневности,
големи и мали здодевности,
стари грижи, стари патила,
стари гревови, стари чесности.
Старо, старо, старо купувам,

RAG-AND-BONE MAN

Old things I buy, I buy old things!
Old tassels, old clothes,
old metal, old loves.
Old things I buy!
I buy old bits and pieces,
nonessential odds and ends,
beat-up shoes, raggedy shirts,
luck that once lucked out.
Old things, old things, old things I buy!
I buy old everyday things,
jealousies of every size,
old vests in your closet,
old pots on your stove,
old soot on your conscience,
old rust on your dreams.
Old things, old things, old things I buy!
I buy old everyday things,
jealousies of every size,
old loves, old luck, old lapses, old lies.
I buy old joys and used-up youth—
old things, old things, old things I buy!

Old things I buy, I buy old things!
Old tassels, old clothes,
old metal, old loves.
I buy old everyday things,
annoyances of every size,
old worries, old sufferings,
old honor, old lies.
Old things, old things, old things I buy!

стари среќи, стари љубови,
стари радости, стари младости,
купувам стари алишта.
Старо, старо, старо купувам,
старо за нови свтралишта.

Old luck, old loves,
old joys, old youth.
I buy old trimmings and clothing.
Old things, old things, old things I buy—
old things for new comings and goings.

ДОЛГО ЖИВЕАМ НА ОВА МЕСТО

Долго живеам на ова место
под кое шуркаат планински извори
и децата ловат пеперуги
а боровите во нема извишеност
ја разлистуваат тишината на вековите.
Долго живеам на ова место
и полека црнеам од времето.
Гледај, велам, гледај каков си:
ни да се препознаеш.
Некогаш овие очи беа длабочини
во кои се нуркаа твоите желби
како жерави во сончевина,
а сега се само две суводолици
за ноќевање на случајните дождови.
Некогаш овие раце беа орачи
во ровката земја на твоите лутања,
а сега личат на врбови прачки
неродници чаталести над водите.
Некогаш велам и ти како децата
си играше со пеперуги в рака
а од нивниот златен прав
цутеа вишните во твојата градина.

Зошто беше толку невнимателен
па дозволи сите да загинат меѓу твоите прсти,
зошто не сфати дека е најголема мудрост
да имаш една жива пеперуга од твоето детство,
една топла ѕвезда на дланката

LONG HAVE I LIVED IN THIS PLACE

Long have I lived in this place,
with mountain springs gushing beneath it,
where the children chase butterflies
and the pine trees in voiceless grandeur
leaf out the silence of the ages.
Long have I lived in this place
and slowly have I darkened from time.
Look, I say, see what you've become:
you cannot even recognize yourself.
These eyes were once deep pools
into which your desires would dive
like cranes in the sunlight.
But now they are merely two hollows
where occasional rains may spend a night.
These arms were once plowmen
in the soft earth of your wanderings.
But now they are like willow branches,
barren and dangling above the waters.
You too, I say, like the children,
once played with butterflies in your hand,
and from their golden dust
cherry trees blossomed in your garden.

Why did you so heedlessly let
them all perish in your fingers?
Why did you not grasp that the greatest wisdom is
to have one living butterfly from your childhood,
one warm star in the palm of your hand,

што ќе го просветли ова место,
ова место каде долго живееш осамен,
долго живееш поцрнет од времето.

that would light up this place,
this place where you have long lived in loneliness,
where you have long lived darkened by time.

КВЕЧЕРИНА

Спиј. Каменот спие. Спијат водите.
Зад ридјето на твоите веѓи
со плашиците на твојот поглед
залез на сонцето.

Спиј. Каменот спие. Спијат водите.
Врз исчадената греда на твојата мисла
ко клупци во селска куќарка
излитени играчки на денот.

Спиј. Каменот спие. Спијат водите.
Над јаболкницата на твоите соништа
над јаболкницата светлотрепетлива
ѕвезди зорници.

NIGHTFALL

Sleep now. The stone is asleep. Sleeping, too, the waters.
Behind the hills of your eyebrows
in the shimmering, timid fish of your eyes—
the setting of the sun.

Sleep now. The stone is asleep. Sleeping, too, the waters.
On the smoky beam of your thoughts
as on the benches in a village house—
the well-worn toys of the day.

Sleep now. The stone is asleep. Sleeping, too, the waters.
Above the apple tree of your dreams,
above the bright-trembling apple tree—
the stars of dawn.

ОЧАЈ ПРЕД ТВРДИНАТА

Тврдино, невидливи воини те пазат.
Стасав и паднав пред тебе на метар.
Ветар и оган, оган и ветар.
Оттука нема враќање назад.

Од грозна немост морници ме лазат.
Очајот само се снове ко волк
низ сурите карпи на тој грозен молк.
Оттука нема враќање назад.

Земјата в срце на грутки се рони,
притиска и тежи, се трупа, ме кани:
Израмни се со мене, земја и ти стани.
Со ветар и оган земјата ме гони.

Рамнодушна, глува за лелек и жртви,
неспособна да жали и суди,
секоја ноќ тврдината ја буди
сонцето на тие што се мртви.

DESPAIR BEFORE THE FORTRESS

Fortress, invisible warriors protect you.
I came and, just a few feet from you, fell.
Fire and wind, wind and fire.
From here there is no going back.

Your terrible silence chills my flesh.
Like a wolf, despair alone is prowling
the ashen rocks of this dread silence.
From here there is no going back.

In my heart, the earth is crumbling to pieces.
It presses, weighs on me; it piles up and dares me:
Be as my equal. You, too, become earthen.
With wind and fire the earth pursues me.

Indifferent, deaf to lost lives and lament,
incapable of pity or condemnation,
night after night the fortress is wakened
by the sunlight of those who are dead.

НЕБИДНИНА

1.

Патував долго, патував цела вечност
од мене до твојата небиднина.
Низ пожари патував, низ урнатини,
низ пепелишта.
По жега, по суша, по невиделина.
Се хранев со лебот на твојата убавина,
пиев од грлото на твојата песна.

Не гледај ги овие црни суводолици
што го параат моето лице –
ми ги подари лицето на земјата.
Не гледај ги овие нерамнини врз плеќите –
ми ги донесе умората на ридјето.

Погледај во овие раце –
два огна,
две реки
темно чекање.
Погледај во овие дланки –
две полиња,
две суши
глуво лелекање.

Патував долго, патував цела вечност
од тебе до мојата небиднина.

NOT-BEING

1.

I traveled a long time, traveled an entire eternity,
from myself to your not-being.
I traveled through fire, through rubble,
through wastes of ash.
In heat, in drought, in utter darkness.
I fed on the bread of your beauty,
I drank from the throat of your song.

Do not look at the dry black gullies
that score my face—
I was given them by the face of the earth.
Do not look at the crookedness of my shoulders—
I received it from the weariness of the hills.

Look at these arms—
two fires,
two rivers
of dark waiting.
Look at these hands—
two fields,
two arid lands
of hollow wailing.

I traveled a long time, traveled an entire eternity,
from you to my not-being.

2.

A сè се случи една ноќ,
ноќ стебла,
ноќ лисје,
ноќ студен ров.
Паднав, потонав во високи треви,
во треви и густа мов.

Се случи тоа една ноќ
вистинито и невистинито
налик на старинска приказна
закопана длабоко во свеста.
Ти дојде и ме однесе како глува поплава,
како матица од подземни места.

И сега сам,
пред овој рид од болка и човештина
на патишта што не ги знам
завивам раскинат од глад и пцости.
Ти дојде како црна вода на болештина
со која се болува довек
од сите проклетства и злости.

3.

Водо непрозирна, водо црна,
ти што откинуваш секој ден
по еден никнат цвет
од каменот на моето чело
и го фрлаш во мрачни бездни
под л'2ката лушпа на своето тело,

2.

And everything happened in a single night,
night of trees,
night of leaves,
night of a cold trench.
I fell, I drowned in tall grass,
in grass and thick moss.

This happened in a single night,
the true and the untrue,
like an ancient story
buried deep in one's consciousness.
You came like a muffled flood and carried me off,
like a welling from places underground.

And now alone
in front of this hill of pain and humanness,
on roads I don't recognize,
ragged from hunger and curses, I howl.
You came like the black water of an illness
in which one is made endlessly sick
by all the scourges, all the evils of the world.

3.

Turbid water, black water,
every day you pluck a new flower
from the stone of my forehead
and toss it into the murky depths
beneath the light skin of your body.
Turbid water, black water,

водо непросирна, водо црна,
кој ти го даде тој облик
на таа мисла прекрасна и страшна
што го обвива моето срце
како стебло млада срна,
кој ти го даде тоа име
водо непросирна, водо црна.

Кој тоа невидлив во мене седи
и пали таен оган,
кој ѝ го руши на крвта sидот,
кој ми го краде слухот,
кој одзема видот,
кој пласт врз пласје неуморен реди,
кој тоа невидлив во мене седи.

4.

Стебло што самееш на ридот,
мако во ровка земја,
кој ти ги даде моите очи
што зреат во сонот на твоите лисје.
Погледу зелен, зелено вишнеење,
кој нè осуди на исто бдеење.
Стебло што самееш на ридот,
Мако во ровка земја,
од каде твоите длабини во мене,
од каде ти во мојата крв.
Кој ги избриша со рака лесна
сите далечини,
сите близини,
кој ни ја досуди таа небиднина
да бидам стебло, да бидеш песна.

who gave you the form
of that beautiful, terrible thought,
which wraps itself around my heart
like a young deer circling a tree?
Who gave you that name,
turbid water, black water?

Who is it who sits invisible inside me
and lights that fire?
Who tears down the wall of my blood?
Who robs me of my hearing?
Who strips me of my sight?
Who tirelessly lays layer upon layer?
Who is it who sits invisible inside me?

4.

Tree alone on the hill,
woundedness in the loose soil,
who gave you my eyes,
which ripen in the dream of your leaves?
Green gaze, green rising,
who condemns us to the same watching?
Tree alone on the hill,
woundedness in the loose soil,
how did your depths come to be inside me,
how did you come to be in my blood?
Whose nimble hand wiped away
all the distances
all the closenesses?
Who condemned us to this not-being,
I to be tree, you to be song?

5.

Жено непозната, жено мудра,
ти што минуваш секогаш спокојна
крај овој прозор на темнината
глува за лелекот,
слепа за очајот,
од каде тоа лажно спокојство,
од каде во тебе мојата крв.
Жено, те чував како тешка тајна
што ќе ја откријам само оној ден
кога ќе се јави зазбивтано крвта
во час на страшна тишина
за смела последна реч,
светла како вишина,
остра како меч.

Од каде во тебе
мојата крв, жено.
Патував долго, патував цела вечност
од нас до нашата небиднина.

5.

Unknown woman, wise woman,
you, always calm, who passes
this window of darkness
deaf to the wailing,
blind to the despair—
where does this false calm come from?
How does my blood come to be inside you?
Woman, I have guarded you like a heavy secret,
which I will not reveal until the day
when my blood appears, gasping,
at an hour of terrible silence,
to speak its brave last words,
bright as the heights,
sharp as a sword.

How does my blood, woman,
come to be inside you?
I traveled a long time, traveled an entire eternity,
from us to our not-being.

ПЕСНАТА И ГОДИНИТЕ

Твоите години и моите години —
два брега,
два камена,
две небиднини.

Твоите години и моите години —
твоите години во мојата мака,
моите години во твоето срце.

Да си благословена најнепозната песно.
Нè изедначуваш во мудроста,
нè израмнуваш во годините.
Да си благословена небидино
во времето што не знае стареење.

Твоите години и моите години —
наши години.

Ти одиш чекор по чекор,
мака по мака
низ моите години,
јас одам чекор по чекор,
мака по мака
низ твоите години.
Нема крај и нема изодување.

Ти си во моето непостоење,
јас во заговорот на твоите соништа.

Да си благословено време

THE SONG AND THE YEARS

Your years and my years—
two shores,
two stones,
two not-beings.

Your years and my years—
your years in my pain,
my years in your heart.

May you be blessed, most unknown song.
You make us equal in wisdom,
you make us even in years.
May you be blessed, not-being,
in a time that knows no aging.

Your years and my years—
our years.

You move step by step,
pain by pain,
through my years.
I move step by step,
pain by pain,
through your years.
There is no end and there is no distance gained.

You inhabit my nonexistence.
I inhabit the conspiracy of your dreams.

May you be blessed, time,

што остануваш исто,
а ние те даруваме со нашите очи
вчера од земја,
денес од небо,
утре од земја и небо.

Да си благословена најнеслутена песно
што нè изедначуваш во мудроста,
што нè израмнуваш во годините.

Твоите години и моите години —
два брега,
два камена,
две небиднини.

who are ever the same.
We offer you our eyes,
yesterday made of earth,
today made of sky,
tomorrow made of earth and sky.

May you be blessed, most unimagined song,
who make us equal in wisdom,
who make us even in years.

Your years and my years—
two shores,
two stones,
two not-beings.

ГЛЕДАЧ ВО ПЕПЕЛТА (1970)

READER OF THE ASHES (1970)

ДОЛГО ДОАЃАЊЕ НА ОГНОТ

THE LONG COMING OF THE FIRE

НОЌТА НА ОГНОТ

Под девет ноќи ѕвезден обрач пука.
А огнот молчи. Пенушка од бука.

Ко чекач сраснат сред скриена чека
тој стои овде од искон, од века.

Ко сува гламја, како црна коба
безвреме трае и годишни доба.

Се палат лисје како лилав темјан.
А огнот молчи. Црн. Потемнет. Земјан.

Се палат лисје како темјан лилав.
А огнот молчи. Ноќ во корен жилав.

THE FIRE'S NIGHT

Beneath nine nights a ring of stars explodes.
But the fire is silent. A beech-tree stump.

Like a hunter lurking in a hidden blind,
it has been here forever, age after age.

Like a dry fungus, like a black omen,
it endures beyond time and from season to season.

Leaves are igniting like violet incense.
But the fire is silent. Black. Shadowy. Earthen.

Like violet incense the leaves ignite.
But the fire is silent. In the sinewy root, night.

ПОВЛЕКУВАЊЕ НА ОГНОТ

Молчи огнот претворен во кора
под бучава на столетна гора.

Запленувач и жртва на пленот
на бел јарбол го качува денот.

Молчи огнот со исушен пламен
под езеро тврдо како камен.

Молчи огнот под бучава тмурна
и се вее ко пепел од урна.

THE FIRE'S RETREAT

The fire is silent, turned to bark,
beneath the roar of an age-old wood.

Predator and victim of its prey,
on a white flagpole it hoists the day.

The fire is silent, its flame dried out,
beneath a lake hard as rock.

The fire is silent beneath the grim roar
and blows in the air like ash from an urn.

ЉУБОВТА НА ОГНОТ

На С. J.

Глув варовник паѓа врз нашите лица.
Се прпелка огнот под него ко птица.

Се прпелка огнот во кафез од време.
На полноќно сонце зрее црно семе.

Сам од себе огнот оган вечен краде,
љубовта на бодеж своја да ја даде.

Греј, полноќно сонце, не запирај, греј.
Еве сам и ранет, иде Прометеј.

Како стрвник стемнет, како земја гладна
го подзеде огнот и изгорен падна.

Песната се стопи како лажно злато.
Подолг е од животот до човека патот.

Сам од себе огнот оган вечен краде
љубовта на бодеж своја да ја даде.

Молчи, молчи, молчи во млада боровина.
Оган и горовина. Оган и горовина.

THE FIRE'S LOVE

To S. J.

Blank limestone falls across our faces.
Like a bird the fire wallows beneath it.

The fire wallows in a cage of time.
Black seed sprouts in the midnight sun.

The fire steals from itself eternal fire
to offer its love upon a dagger.

Burn, midnight sun, do not stop burning.
Prometheus comes, alone and wounded.

Like a dark bird of prey, like hungry soil,
he seizes the fire, is burned and falls.

The song like fool's gold melted away.
The road to man is longer than life.

The fire steals from itself eternal fire
to offer its love upon a dagger.

Silent, silent, be silent in the young firwood.
Fire and furnace. Fire and furnace.

ДОЛГО ДОАЃАЊЕ НА ОГНОТ

1.

Тука е тој оган под овие улави води,
под овој бигор и зло самото што се плоди.

Под овие води тешки и зрели
тримеѓница црна црно што ги дели.

Под овој венец од сончеви глави,
под оваа далга со карпи што се дави.

Под овој екот, заклињања и злоби,
и ова дрво на брегот од дамнина што коби.

Тука е тој оган под оваа кожа,
под овие тримеѓници, овие три ножа.

Секогаш и сегде семожен и морен,
ѕвезда е во срце и мрак е во корен.

Копај,
ископај го.

2.

Од вруток до уток,
од грст до крст.

Од подземнина до изземнина,

THE LONG COMING OF THE FIRE

1.

The fire is here, beneath these mad waters,
beneath this limestone and self-sowing evil.

Beneath these waters heavy and ripened
three black boundaries blackly divide them.

Beneath this wreath from sunheads wrought,
beneath this wave choking on rocks.

Beneath this thunder, sworn oaths and malice,
and this tree on the bank with its age-old menace.

The fire is here, underneath this hide,
beneath these three boundaries, these three knives.

Always and everywhere all-powerful and weary,
a star in the heart, and in the root, darkness.

Dig,
dig it up.

2.

From headspring to delta,
from fist to cross.

From underground to frozen ground,

од брат до тат.

Од светилка до бесилка,
од реч до меч.

Копај,
ископај го.

3.

Не ќе го ископаш ти никогаш тука.
Еве го сраснат со прастара бука.

Меѓу три стебла се ниша во лулка.
Ветар е црвен во секоја булка.

Воин во црква на икона стара.
Исчезнат говор себе што се бара.

Еве го, клекнат ко занесен голтар
својот збор го длаби во резба за олтар.

Во себе копај, под својата кожа,
под трите лузни, под трите ножа.

4.

Копај,
ископај го.

Од селишта до пепелишта,
од боска до коска.

from brother to brute.

From glow to gallows,
from word to sword.

Dig,
dig it up.

3.

Here you will never dig it up.
See how it's fused to the ancient beech tree.

It rocks in a cradle between three trees.
In every poppy a red wind blows.

It's the warrior in an icon in an old church.
It's a long-vanished speech in search of itself.

See how it kneels like a beggar enraptured
as it gouges its word in the carving for an altar.

Dig into yourself, beneath your own hide,
beneath the three scars, beneath the three knives.

4.

Dig,
dig it up.

From villages to cinders,
from breast to bone.

Од бог до глог,
од жетва до клетва.

Од белег до лелек,
од канија до востанија.

Копај,
ископај го.

5.

Не ќе го ископаш никогаш ни со грабежи диви.
Ни мртвите се мртви ни живите живи.

Крстот им беше лесен, пепелта не им е лесна.
Мртвите ќе умрат тогаш кога и нивната песна.

Не им е тежок гробот мртвите кајшто лежат.
Песните што ги пеат на живите им тежат.

Не ќе го ископаш огнот ни да векуваш тука.
Тоа е тој светец од икона што пука.

Тоа е тој камен на сите мртви зглавје,
таа трпеза ѕвездена, таа болест и здравје.

Тоа е таа магија, таа крв чуда што прави,
што лекува од рани и што симиња глави.

Под своите лузни копај, под ножот што те служи,
огнот е во твоите очи пожар од бунт на ружи.

From god to hawthorn,
from harvest to curse.

From mark to lament,
from scabbard to revolt.

Dig,
dig it up.

5.

Never will you dig it up, not with wild thieving.
The dead are not dead and the living not living.

For them the cross was light, but not light the ashes.
The dead will only die the day their song passes.

For the dead who lie there, the grave is not heavy.
But the songs that they sing weigh hard on the living.

Here, long though you live, you won't dig up the fire.
It is that saint who bursts from the icon.

It is that stone where the dead make their pillow,
that starry feast, that health and that illness.

It is that magic, that wonder-working blood,
which repairs your wounds and severs your head.

Dig beneath your scars, beneath the knife that serves you;
in your eyes the fire blazes with the roses' insurgence.

6.

Копај,
ископај го.

Својата последна клетва реките ќе ја речат,
и ќе секнат, ќе престанат да течат.

Небото ќе се сруши.
Ќе се стркалаат планини. Ќе завладеат суши.

Ќе се измешаат ѕвезди и ѕверови, отрови и ниви,
и нема да се знае повеќе ни кои се мртви ни кои се живи.

Копај,
ископај го.

7.

Додека под себе копаш над тебе тој ќе се јави
и една мртва глава на рамо ќе ти стави.

Огнот низ краишта тајни заслепен ќе те носи,
и нема да се прашаш каде си, кој си, што си.

Овде е, во овој корен, во овој молк што свети
и нема својата светлина никогаш да ја сети.

Тој на секое дрво со секој мртов виси.
Тоа сме ние, тоа сум јас и тоа ти си.

6.

Dig,
dig it up.

The rivers will utter their final vow
and then run dry and cease to flow.

The heavens will come crashing down.
The mountains will tumble. Deserts will reign.

Stars will mix with beasts, toxins with tillage,
and none will know who is dead and who is living.

Dig,
dig it up.

7.

As you dig beneath you, it will appear above you
and place a death's head upon your shoulder.

The fire will carry you blinded through secret realms,
and where or who or what you are, you will not ask yourself.

It is here, in this root, in this silence which shines,
and yet its own light it never will sense.

It hangs with every dead body on every tree.
This is us, this is you, this is me.

И кога таков личи на глас што сам се гаси,
од некоја вишина глува повторно ќе ти се гласи.

8.

Во себе копај, под својата кожа,
под црното сонце на трите ножа.

Тука е тој оган под овие улави води,
во оваа утроба гладна гладен збор што роди.

А може и ѕверот во дувло да го скроти,
да раскине, да здроби, да убие и сплоти.

Со него за убост поубав е цветот,
без него за цел свет посиромав светот.

Крстот ни е лесен, пепелта не ни е лесна,
мртвите ќе умрат со нас и со нашата песна.

And if it seems in such form like a voice fading out,
it will call to you again from a distant height.

8.

Dig into yourself, beneath your own hide,
beneath the black sun of the three knives.

The fire is here, beneath these waters gone mad,
in this hungry womb which bears a hungry word.

But it also can tame the wild beast in his den,
it can rend and crush and kill and join.

With it beauty is added to the beauty of the flower;
without it the world is an entire world poorer.

For us the cross is light, but the ashes—no light thing.
The dead will die with us and with the song we sing.

ГЛЕДАЧ ВО ПЕПЕЛТА

READER OF THE ASHES

ГРОЗОМОР

Тука се раѓаат сами и гаснат сите нешта.
Огромен камен. Лузна. Нејасен немушт збор.
Пролетта му е мајка и маќеа зла и вешта.
Пепел на сонот, сон на пепелта. Грозомор.

Го пијат суши, дождови црни го цедат,
ден со ноќ го трупа, пласт со пласт,
а врз неговата кора во ’рбетник се редат
закостенети сенки од диво месо и страст.

Тука ветришта пиштат и темни сеништа вијат,
тука е првиот злочин и грев и казна и прекор.
Тука и човек и ѕвер во едно дувло спијат
и детето го оди својот незаоден чекор.

Врз него расне лебот од горчлив длабок корен,
па затоа е сув, и сладок, и пече како пламен.
Песно, ако те допре некој испосник морен
прими го да ти биде во горењето рамен.

О ружо в грло, о змијогрозд в усни,
див апеж во крвта со себе што спори,
о земјо на отрови смртоносно вкусни,
каменот во пламен се тркала. Гори. Гори. Гори.

Тука се раѓаат сите нешта и тука гаснат сами.
Огромен камен. Лузна. Нејасен немушт збор.
Пролетта му е мајка и маќеа што мами,
пепел на сонот, сон на пепелта. Грозомор.

HORRORDEATH

Here all things are born and die on their own.
A great stone. A scar. A mumbled, muted word.
Spring is its mother and stepmother, wicked and shrewd.
Ashes of the dream, dream of the ashes. Horrordeath.

Droughts drink it, black rains sift it,
days heap it with night, layer upon layer,
while down its hide the vertebrae stiffen
with ossified shadows of raw flesh and rage.

Here winds are whistling and dark ghosts wail,
here the first crime, sin, punishment, rebuke.
Here sleep human and beast in one lair,
and the little child takes her first stumbling step.

The bread on it grows from a root deep and bitter,
so it is dry and sweet and sears like a flame.
Song, should some weary hermit accost you,
accept him as your own: he burns the same.

O rose in the throat, snakeberry in the mouth,
wild itch of the blood with itself contending;
O land of delectable, deadly poisons,
the blazing boulder rolls. Burning. Burning. Burning.

Here all things, on their own, are born and die.
A great stone. A scar. A mumbled, muted word.
Spring is its mother and stepmother, full of lies.
Ashes of the dream, dream of the ashes. Horrordeath.

ЗЛАТЕН КРУГ НА ВРЕМЕТО

Старинска ѕвездо, ѕвездо на пророци и чуда, —
распрсни се во стихот, потони во најцрн мрак.
Повеќе трае во крвта оваа светлина луда
и овој невидлив пламен што нема ни име ни знак.

Сениште ѕвездено, ѕвездо на студена мора, —
исчезни со сите наречници со сите митови падни.
Под ова стебло од зборови зараснати во столетна кора
се пали страшен оган и горат корени гладни.

Кој си ти што идеш со лузни од правта на векот далечен,
со едно дамна во неврат отшумено време,
и место лика на некој очајник жален
носиш суров закон за себе и своето племе?

Гласи се со вии од молк, проговори со поглед нем,
засводен во својот говор со јазли семоќно власни,
и како ненужен воин со очи од црнозем
обѕрни се во кругот златен и победоносен згасни.

Старинска ѕвездо, ѕвездо на пророци и чуда, —
распрсни се во стихот, потони во најдлабок збор,
додека трае во крвта оваа светлина луда
овој подземен оган, овој непрегор.

THE GOLDEN CIRCLE OF TIME

Ancient star, star of prophecy and miracles,
explode into the poem, sink into the darkest gloom.
Longer in the blood does this mad light linger,
and this invisible flame without sign or name.

Ghost of a star, star of a cold nightmare,
vanish with all the fates, fall with all the fables.
Beneath this tree of words encrusted with age-old bark,
a terrible fire is sparking and hungry roots are burning.

Who are you who comes here scarred by the dust of a distant era
and with an age that ended long ago never to return—
coming not in the form of some poor wretch despairing,
but bringing instead cruel law for yourself and for your clan?

Sound out with a howl of silence, speak with a mute gaze,
in your speech overvaulted with all-powerful knots,
and like a useless soldier with chernozem eyes
look back at the golden circle and triumphantly burn out.

Ancient star, star of prophecy and miracles,
explode into the poem, sink into the deepest word,
until this mad light no longer lingers in the blood,
this netherworldly fire, this undying heat.

ТАЖАЧКА ОД ОНАА СТРАНА НА ЖИВОТОТ

Се искачив над врвот од болот.
Човек сум. А што е човек?
Пред мене празнина, зад мене празнина.
Празнина што сама се пали.

Од онаа страна на животот,
жив распнат со слепи јазли.
Се искачив над врвот од болот.
Тој ден. Црнден. По црни скали.

Се искачив над врвот од болот.
Од онаа страна на животот
од онаа страна на себе си,
на сè неизговорено,
сè што е недогорено,
од онаа страна на водата,
од онаа страна на врутокот,
од онаа страна на коренот.

Стопи се грутко, истечи водо,
прелеј се чашо лелејска
за сите градови во овој град,
за сите црнини во оваа црнина.
Кажете кого да обвинувам.
Кого да жалам, кажете!
О дете што те нема —
мојата црнина твоја прегрнина.

Мојата црнина твоја прегрнина,
твојата темнина моја подземнина.

LAMENT FROM THE OTHER SIDE OF LIFE

I climbed above the summit of the pain.
I am human. But what is a human?
Emptiness before me, emptiness behind me.
Emptiness that catches fire.

From the other side of life,
with strong knots crucified alive,
I climbed above the summit of the pain.
That day. Blackday. Up black stairs.

I climbed above the summit of the pain.
From the other side of life,
from the other side of myself,
of everything not spoken,
everything not burned away,
from the other side of the water,
from the other side of the wellspring,
from the other side of the root.

Dissolve, clump of clay, flow out, water,
overflow, cup of keening,
for all the cities of this city,
all the grievings of this grieving.
Tell me who to blame,
who to feel sorry for? Tell me!
O child who is no more—
my grieving, your embrace.

My grieving, your embrace,
your darkness, my netherworld.

Земјо олелио, земјо пустелио,
од мртов плач израсната
земјо обѕрни се, земјо разгрни се.

Земи ја оваа зеница
земи ја оваа пшеница
на твоја дланка згасната.

Земи ме, земјо, или врати ме,
врати ме подолу од овој врв,
подолу од онаа страна на животот,
човечки сили дај ми пак.
О земјо, на земја врати ме.
Човек сум, човек да страдам,
да најдам камен жив да се вградам
на некој мост во некој лак.

O earth of keening, earth of desert,
from dead weeping grown,
earth, look around, earth, uncover yourself.

Take this eye,
take this wheat
in your withered hand.

Take me, earth, or bring me back,
bring me back below this summit,
below the other side of life,
return my human powers to me.
O earth, bring me back to earth.
I am human, meant as a human to suffer,
to find stone, to wall myself up alive
in an arch on some bridge.

АКО ТИ НЕДОСТАСУВА СВЕТЛИНА

Ако ти недостасува светлина
земај ме.
Ноќ да сум ноќ ќе изгорам
ќе те разденам.

Ако и љубов ти недостасува
земај ме.
Црнките на ноќта ќе ги ископам
ѕвезда да се огледаш, да огрееш.

Ако ти недостасува омраза
и тогаш земај ме.
Пекол ми вие под срце
пекол вековиште.

Ако ти недостасува светлина
земај ме.

Ако пак јас ти недостасувам
што сум ти!
Без да те гледам во недоглед
без да изгорам.

IF THERE ISN'T ENOUGH LIGHT FOR YOU

If there isn't enough light for you,
take me.
That I may be night, a night that burns away
to bring you day.

And if there isn't enough love for you,
take me.
I will dig out the pupils in the eyes of the night
that you mirror a star and shine.

If there isn't enough hate for you,
even then, take me.
Hell is weaving beneath my heart
a hell for all eternity.

If there isn't enough light for you,
take me.

But if there isn't enough me for you,
what am I to you?
Except that I gaze at you endlessly,
except that I burn away.

НЕВРЕМЕ

Како ме носи реката, како ме фрла
од едно до друго езеро, од една до друга жед.
Најсудбоносно пеат рибите со неми грла,
тие што вечно кружат ко воден сончоглед.

Слези долу по скалите на оваа кула,
распретај ја жарта под крилата на водната птица
бранот на најмалиот цвет сите векови таму ги лула
и талка огромни сеништа од некои дамнешни лица.

Рика утробата, ко густо небо секавица ја кине,
светот се корне, пукаат старите оски,
и сè се урива, сè пропаѓа и гине
пред срните на бранот како пред расцутени боски.

Плачи водо, завивај утробо, завивај кугло запалена.
Времето невреме вистинско е време.
Под тебе земјата лежи од умора премалена
и црн коњаник иде плодот да си го земе.

TEMPEST

How the river carries me, how it tosses me along
from one lake to another, one thirst to another.
With silent throats the fish incant a vatic song—
they who circle endlessly like a sunflower of water.

Go from this tower, descend the stair,
stoke the embers beneath the wings of the waterbird—
the smallest blossom's ripple rocks all the centuries there
and moves the looming shadows of faces long departed.

The depths of the earth roar, like dense cloud rent by lightning,
the world is uprooted, the old axles crack with doom,
all is shattered, collapsing, everything is dying
before the deer on the wave as before breasts in bloom.

Weep, water! Depths, wail! Wail, planet ablaze!
Weather that rages is weather in truth.
Beneath you the earth lies exhausted and dazed,
and a dark horseman comes to gather his fruit.

НОЌЕН ИЗВОР

Загледан
во ноќен извор
како во урочен лик,
што најде
што откри,
какви огнови стопи,
па не чу
како паѓа птицата
од сопствен крик
или од темјан на вода
смртно што ја опи.

Загледан
во тоа огледало
срцето што ти го скова
во какви длабини слезе,
од која вода се напи,
дали те зароби звукот
на магија нова,
во мртво море
од камен луд ли стапи,

па сега
во ноќен извор
како во своја слика
го бараш
оној летач
сурово што ќе ти суди.

NIGHT SPRING

Staring
into a spring at night
as into a face bewitched,
what did you find,
what did you discover,
what fires did you put out,
yet did not hear
the bird as it fell
struck by its own cry,
or by the fatally intoxicating
incense of the water.

Staring
into this mirror
that rivets your heart,
to what depths did you descend,
what water slaked your thirst,
were you captivated by the sound
of some new magic,
did you step from a stone of madness
into a dead sea,

so that now
in a spring at night
as in your own image
you search
for that flier who will
cruelly judge you.

И нити гледаш нешто
ни слушаш
како те вика
славејот
во крвта твоја
пеколот што го буди.

And you see nothing,
nor do you hear
the nightingale
that calls to you
and in your blood
awakens hell.

АВГУСТ

Лежам под стеблото на ноќта, во август што умира и пее
со цвет од пепел на згасната гроза.
Од челото како од црница набабрува и ми зрее
од гроздови ѕвездената лоза.

Лежам во ноќта на август за земја прикован со теме.
Дали ќе додржат, дали ќе ме запрат
овие неуморни воини од билје и семе,
од треви, корени и папрат.

Лежи и чекај тука. Неподвижен, карпосан лежи,
што ако ноќта те пие, што ако ветар те шиба.
Рибарите на твојот поглед плетат невидливи мрежи,
во бездната на твоето чекање сонува златна риба.

Лежам и знам, август е и сè се мени.
Златните зрна на гроздот ко едри зеници гаснат.
Темното полноќно сонце патува кон својот зенит.
А јас останувам заробен во треви и со папрат сраснат.

AUGUST

Beneath the tree of night I lie, in August, which is dying and singing
in a flower of ash from the burned-out horror.
From my forehead, as if from black soil, a vine of stars is springing,
heavy with ripening, swelling clusters.

In the August night I lie, my head riveted to the earth.
Will they stop me, will they continue to hold me—
these tireless soldiers of seeds and herbs,
of grass and roots and ferns and foliage?

Lie here and wait. Be still. Be a stone.
So what if night drinks you and you're lashed by the wind?
The fishermen in your eyes weave nets unseen:
in the depths of your waiting a golden fish dreams.

I lie here and know: it is August and everything's changing.
The golden grapes like widened pupils lose their fire.
The dark sun of midnight proceeds to its zenith.
But I remain captive in grass, cemented to ferns.

ГЛЕДАЧ ВО ПЕПЕЛТА

Изгасни песно во огнот што го запали сама.
Прска зборот и исчезнува во пепел од кремен.
Гледачу во пепелта, ја препозна ли во неа исконската драма
што доаѓа од дното на овој извор темен.

Песно, те откинав од клунот на птица во крвта што ми лета,
од црвеното небо на запалените вени,
од тие далноводи на два непомирливи света,
тие изгрејсонца со неодгатнати мени.

Те откинав од гневот на иконите, тие неразбирливи гами,
од громот врз копјето на воинот со камен што е сраснат,
од сонот на тие повисоки што се од сонот што ги мами,
и што се раѓаат пак откако еднаш згаснат.

Сега сме два света, два врага, две завојувани страни,
сега сме војна без излез и кама против кама.
Кој е победен? Кој победник? Кој со изгрев на осмислени рани?
Изгасни песно во огнот што го запали сама.

READER OF THE ASHES

Burn out, song, in the fire you ignited.
The word explodes, disappears, into ashes of flint.
Reader of the ashes, did you note the primordial drama
arising from the depths of this dark origin?

I snatched you, song, from the beak of the bird flying in my blood,
from the red sky of my veins inflamed and pulsating,
from the wires of two irreconcilable worlds,
those sunrises with their indecipherable phases.

I snatched you from the wrath of icons, from those illegible gammas,
from the thunder off the spear of the stone-fused warrior,
from the dream of those loftier than the dream that betrays them
and those who are reborn after once having perished.

Now we are two worlds, two adversaries, two warring sides,
now we are war with no exit, dagger to dagger.
Who loses? Who wins? Who, with the dawning of wounds clarified?
Burn out, song, in the fire you ignited.

ЦРНИ КОЊАНИЦИ, БЕЛИ КОЊИЦИ

BLACK HORSEMEN, WHITE RIDERS

ЕЗЕРО

Биј далго. Врти вртушко. По брегот биј.
Ѕвоно од ветар и светлина ѕвони.
Ти надоаѓаш, езеро, а твојот непресушен виј
гасне заедно со брегот што се рони.

Тука си, а ќе те загубам стиснато зад некој рид,
само си, а се отвараш во мене како школка,
и како во суводолица пропаѓаш во мојот вид
со една нејасна далечна болка.

Тогаш разбирам, езеро: пак долго ќе те нема
и не знам кој пат веќе пак ќе ми се стори
дека си оган тајно што се зема
нечие срце, крв нечија да гори.

А ти надоаѓаш со закана, со виј, со блесок,
и од сѐ што пред тебе залуд ќе се скрие
останува само сенка, само песок.
Песок на брегот стрвно што те пие.

И ја слутам веќе таа непрегледна суша,
тој предел нем, зараснат со црна кора
што место тебе жедни врутоци слуша
како тркалање на два тешки збора.

О езеро, ти надоаѓаш а брегот со тебе се рони.
Скриј се зад твојата убавина. Навлечи лик од виј.
Водата сѐ ќе сознае, водата сѐ ќе сони.
Биј далго. Врти вртушко. Езеро биј.

THE LAKE

Pound, wave. Whirlwind, whirl. Pound the shore.
Ring out, bell of light and wind!
You are rising, lake, but your bottomless howl
dwindles together with the crumbling sand.

You are here, but I'll lose you pressed behind some hill;
alone, but like a shell you open within me,
and into my sight you fall as into a dry ravine
with a kind of pang obscure and distant.

Then I know, lake: again you'll be gone a long time,
and for the millionth time again I will feel
that you are fire, a secretly stolen flame
to burn someone's heart, to burn someone's blood.

But you rise with menace, with howling, with splendor,
and whatever might try in vain to escape you,
nothing will remain except shadow and sand—
the sand on the shore that thirstily drinks you.

And already that limitless drought I sense,
that unspeaking realm overgrown with black crust,
which listens not to you but to thirsting springs
as if to the rolling of two heavy words.

O lake, you are rising and with you the shore crumbles.
Hide behind your beauty. Take the shape of a howl.
The water will grasp everything, the water will dream it.
Pound, wave. Whirlwind, whirl. Pound, lake, pound.

ЕЗЕРО КРАЈ МАНАСТИРОТ

Црни коњаници, бели коњици.
Со лик на светци — на ѕидот сурови војници.

Бран до бранови. Коњ до коњи. Арапин црн ги гони.
Моме застанато на брегот, брегот се рони.

На брегот занишан девојка млада.
Сонцето се спушта на копје од балада.

Ветар коњаник, ветрови коњици.
Врсници сме, водо, од два света двојници.

Водо што извираш од срце на фреска,
грлото ми е од сонце, очите гроздови од треска.

На брегот занишан девојка млада.
Сонцето гине на копје од балада.

Кај исчезна зборот што семожен те бара
да засвечи во тебе како златна пара.

Водата се враќа во фреска на ѕидот.
Со неа и зборот и пламенот на ридот.

THE LAKE BY THE MONASTERY

Black horsemen, white riders.
Saintly figures—on the wall, cruel soldiers.

Wave to waves. Horse to horses. Pursued by the Moor.
On the shore, a girl. On the crumbling shore.

A young maiden stands on the shifting shoreline.
The sun is descending on the spear of a ballad.

The wind a horseman; the riders, winds.
We're the same age, water—from two worlds, twins.

Water, you spring from the heart of the fresco;
my throat from the sun; my eyes, grapes of fever.

A young maiden stands on the shifting shoreline.
The sun is dying on the spear of a ballad.

Where has the all-powerful word gone which seeks you,
to reverberate inside you like a golden coin?

The water is returning to the fresco on the wall.
And with it the word and the flame on the hill.

НОЌ НАД ЕЗЕРОТО КРАЈ МАНАСТИРОТ

Езерото секна, истече со видот.
Водата се врати во фреска на ѕидот.

Лежиме во дното на котлина празна.
Ти си сè што имам: награда и казна.

Расцутува ноќта како црно лале.
Ти личиш на црква сред карпи, на кале.

Па ги гледам само двете твои ѕвона,
две школки во мрежа, два кошмарни сона.

Како црно лале цути ноќта црна.
На врв бели ѕвона две бакарни зрна.

Ѕвони, ѕвони, ѕвони, со подземен рев.
Фатени сме, песно, во првиот грев.

Истечува огнот, истечува видот.
Скаменета везба во фреска на ѕидот.

NIGHT OVER THE LAKE BY THE MONASTERY

The lake has dried up, has faded from sight.
The water has returned to the fresco on the wall.

We lie at the bottom of an empty valley.
You are all I have: my reward and punishment.

The night is opening like a black tulip.
You, a church among the rocks, a fortress.

I see just your two bells and nothing more,
two shells in a net, two dreams—nightmares.

Like a black tulip the black night opens.
Atop the white bells, two seeds of copper.

Toll, toll, toll with a netherworldly din.
We are trapped, song, in the first sin.

The fire is going out, sight is fading.
In the fresco on the wall, stone-still the embroidery.

ЦРНО СОНЦЕ

BLACK SUN

ЦРНО СОНЦЕ

1.

Ни исток имаш, црно сонце, ни имаш запад,
ни небо за молитва ни земја за напад.

И секој што ќе посака да ти се напие од сјајот
изгнаник е од пеколот и изгнаник од рајот.

Тревите се веднат, дрвјето трчаат боси
пред твојот цвет што гори и црна пепел носи.

Црно сонце, птицо преправена во ѕвезда,
кој мисли дека те сфатил не знае што е бездна.

Црно сонце, црно без исток и запад,
црно сонце за жедни на брегот што ќе стапат.

2.

Од која незнајна земја, како долета тука
о црно сонце, птицо во живо дрво што клука.

Кој маѓесник те прати, со каква тајна сила
ѕуницо над триста Волги и преку триста Нила.

Каков е тој небесен појас, таа шарена лента
од сите темни галаксии па до нас — два континента.

BLACK SUN

1.

You have no east, black sun, nor have you any west,
neither sky for praying to nor land for waging war.

And anyone who desires to drink fully of your glory
is banished from hell and banished from heaven.

The meadow grass droops, the trees run barefoot
from your flower, which burns and carries black ash.

Black sun, bird dressed in the guise of a star,
whoever thinks they know you knows not the abyss.

Black sun, black with neither east nor west,
black sun for the thirsty who step onto the shore.

2.

From what unknown land did you end up here,
black sun, bird pecking at a living tree?

What sorcerer sent you, by what secret might,
rainbow over three hundred Volgas, across three hundred Niles?

What celestial belt is this, what bright-colored ribbon that runs
from all the dark galaxies to us—two continents?

Зар да те истрадам сега пред да знам како се страда,
пред да те видам како вселенска барикада.

О црно сонце, песно, о кој ли тоа те става
на плеќи да те носам место својата глава.

3.

Каде ме водиш сега, која ли пештера глува
сè што ќе биде наше ќе знае да го чува.

Ѕвездите гледаат во нас, а ѕвездите се слепи.
Ние сме само на светот како две сраснати крепи.

Кој тоа над нас стои, кој тоа над нас ѕида
за да нè закопа живи во мртва пирамида.

О песно, земјо, жено, о живот и смрт ведно
сè што ми носиш денес, сам ќе го испијам жедно.

Ни исток имаш, црно сонце, ни имаш запад,
Попусто те молам со молитва за напад.

Must I suffer the pain of you now, before I know what suffering is,
before I see you as a barricade across the universe?

Black sun, O song, who was it who set you here,
for me to carry on my shoulders in place of my head?

3.

Where are you leading me now? What soundless cave
will know how to safeguard all that we will have?

The stars are gazing at us, but the stars are blind.
We are alone in the world, like two rocks conjoined.

Who is it standing over us? Who lays brick on brick,
to bury us alive in a lifeless pyramid?

O song, land, woman, O life and death at once,
whatever you bring me today I will thirstily drink up.

You have no east, black sun, nor have you any west,
In vain I pray to you—with a prayer of war.

ПАК ЦРНО СОНЦЕ

Од какво измислено царство, од каква раскошна гробница,
навечер што те прибира а наутро гони,
доаѓаш, црно сонце, и црни истураш дождови
како последна закана на светот што му ѕвони.

Ѕвер со ѕвер ли се јаде, вејка со вејка стара,
стебло во стебло ли удира, корен во корења диви,
ѕвезда опашица со оган небото ли го пара,
војува ли земја со небо, војуваат ли мртви со живи.

Какво е тоа измислено царство, таа гробница на ветар што дува,
од која триглаво сениште триж стрвно во нас гледа,
во овој простор од злостор, вода без вододелница, вода сува,
во оваа црница собрана во една човечка педа.

Каква е таа земја што ѝ го даваме нашето име
препишано од сите ѕидини, од сите мрачнини и висје,
црно сонце, црно и лете и зиме,
тука сме обата покриени со сонцопадно лисје.

AGAIN BLACK SUN

From what imagined kingdom do you come, from what ornate tomb,
which takes you in at nightfall and casts you out at morning—
where are you from, black sun, who pour down black rains,
which toll for the world like the last bell of warning?

Is beast devouring beast? Are old branches colliding,
trunk striking trunk, wild root against root?
Does a falling star rip the sky open with fire?
Does earth war with heaven, the living with the dead?

What is that imagined kingdom, that tomb of gusting wind,
where a three-headed shade thrice-hungrily eyes us,
in this place of crime, of dry water without watershed,
in this black soil contained in a single human handbreadth?

What is this land that we bestow our name on,
copied from all the walls, all the darknesses and heights?
Black sun, who are black in winter and summer,
here both of us are covered in leaves of fallen sunlight.

И УШТЕ ЕДНАШ ЦРНО СОНЦЕ

Тука сè на тебе смртоносно личи.
И овој катран расфрлан врз ридјето.
И оваа смола
што се цеди низ грлото на три суви дола.
И тагата на песот низ приградските населби што квичи
и таа на тебе личи.

И оваа карпа вода што ја плиска,
вода што се подава како жена
во преграб да ја фати
оној за жедта нескротена со живот што ќе плати.
И оваа модрина скржава и недостижно блиска.
И оваа карпа над неа што ја плиска.

И овие лозја и лозници. И вина,
наточени од усвит, од припек, од врелина.
И суша.
И овој камен со збигорена душа.
И трите, црно сонце, нашите три сина
жедни сред лозја, лозници и вина.

И овој ѕвонарник во густите лески
што моли и проколнува.
И рането ечи.
И секој што доаѓа во мир да се лечи.
И очите ископани од старите фрески.
И овој ѕвонарник во густите лески.

Тука сè на тебе смртоносно личи.
И овој катран расфрлан врз ридјето.

AND YET AGAIN BLACK SUN

Here everything lethally bears your likeness.
Even this tar scattered across the hills.
And this resin
seeping from the gorge of three dry rivers.
And the sorrow of the dog whimpering through the outer districts—
even this bears your likeness.

And this cliff the water is lapping against,
water that surrenders itself like a woman,
wanting the embrace
of him who will pay with his life for unbridled thirst.
And this blueness, stinting and unattainably close.
And this cliff above it, against which it laps.

And these vineyards and vines. And wines
poured from incandescence, from scorch, from heat.
And drought.
And this stone with a soul turned to chalk.
And these three, O black sun, our own three sons,
who thirst amid vineyards and vines and wines.

And this belltower in a thick hazel forest,
which is praying and cursing.
And echoing woundedness.
And everyone who comes here to be healed in peace.
And the gouged-out eyes in the ancient frescoes.
And this belltower in a thick hazel forest.

Here everything lethally bears your likeness.
Even this tar scattered across the hills.

И оваа смола.
И над нив Големата ѕвездена кола.
И песот дури низ приградските населби што квичи
и тој во тагата на тебе личи . . .

И оваа земја метежна а јасна.
И оваа суша. И врелина.
И мора.
И трите мои рани — трите неизречени збора.
О црно сонце, огну на есента касна,
светлина капе врз нас од ѕвезда што одамна згасна.

And this resin.
And the starry Great Wagon above them.
And the dog whimpering all through the outer districts—
even he in his sorrow bears your likeness . . .

And this land, turbulent but clear.
And this drought. And heat.
And nightmare.
And my three wounds—three words never uttered.
O black sun, late autumn's fire,
light trickles down on us from a long-burned-out star.

ПОРАНЕШНИ ПЕСНИ

EARLIER POEMS

Од
СО НАШИ РАЦЕ (1950)

From
WITH OUR HANDS (1950)

ОЧИ

Три дена на раце те носевме збрана,
со тага и болка во погледот срчен,
и секоја капка од твојата рана
ко крвава жар ми капеше в срце.

Другарите беа и морни и гладни,
со згорени грла и свиени плеќи,
со тап бол се впија во очите ладни
и жалеа оти не ќе пламнат веќе.

Но јас знаев оти пак ќе вивнат в жарој
и борците под нив ќе цветат и раснат,
в студените утра ќе греат ко сонце
и никогаш нема да стивнат и згаснат.

Последната вечер в планинското село,
кај борците беа во дрипава дреа,
со пликови жешки на стапалки тешки,
и смрштени чела — згасени, мразни
ко нивните пушки укочени, празни,
и нечујно, глуво, ко здушена река
се точеше шепот од уво до уво:
"Утре, друже, в зори, страшен бој нѐ чека,
а ние сме малку — сал неколку души . . ."
И кога ко игла ти прободе уши —
ти растресе снага и размолска тага,
со луњени очи широки и волни
ги расече в ноќта здивените молњи!—
Ко тогаш, ко тогаш, о другарко, помниш —
в смрзнатата вечер на пролетта рана,

EYES

Three days we carried you gathered in our arms,
in our gleaming eyes, pain and sorrow,
and every drop that dripped from your wound
fell on my heart like a bleeding ember.

Our comrades were exhausted and hungry,
their throats burning, their shoulders hunched;
with dull pain they peered into your cold eyes,
fearing that never would they blaze again.

But I knew that once more they would flare into flame
and beneath them our fighters would flourish and grow,
on cold mornings they would bring warmth like the sun
and never would dim, never burn out.

On that last night in the mountain village,
our fighters all in tattered clothes,
their feet heavy and stinging with blisters,
their faces worried, as worn out and cold
as their rifles were numb and empty—
there flowed like the sound of a distant river
from ear to ear a barely audible whisper:
"Comrade, fierce battle awaits us at dawn,
and we are so few—just a handful of souls."
When this news like a needle bore into your ear,
your body started shaking, sorrow flashing,
and with eyes of storm, wide and free,
you split the night with furious lightning.
Like that time before—you remember, dear comrade—
that freezing night in early spring,

кај нашата младост и првата радост
ја косеше луто куршумната слана,
а ти чело збрчка, ко тигрица рипна
и летна во ноќта крвава и црна, —
со своите очи што ригаа пламен
ги растопи часкум челичните зрна . . .

И после! И после — в последната вечер . . .
Јас нејќам да мислам што потаму стана!
Сал помнам те изви крвавата рана,
прошталниот шепот ти замрзна в усни,
но гореа очи под веѓите густи!
Со нивниот пламен и со клетва света,
на заседа тргнав сред мојата чета.

А утринта кога зрив чела ни спраши
ти не беше веќе в редовите наши,
но скипеа борци со одмазда жолчна,
и видов! о видов — кога бојот почна
развихреа сите со твојата сила —
ко елени брзи и лесни ко птица.

А твоите очи се искреа гневно
на нивните потни, распалени лица . . .

Три дена на раце те носевме збрана,
со тага и болка во погледот срчен,
и секоја капка од твојата рана
ко крвава жар ми капеше в срце.

when our youth, when the very first joy we shared,
was mowed down in anger by a hoarfrost of shells,
and with a grimace you leapt like a tigress
into the black and bleeding night—
in an instant, with eyes spewing fire,
you melted the deadly pellets of iron.

And later! And later, on that last night—
I don't want to think about what came next!
I only recall how the bleeding wound wrenched you,
and your whispered farewell froze on your lips,
but your eyes still burned beneath your thick lashes!
With their flame and a sacred oath in my breast,
I left with the others into the ambush.

In the morning, as gunpowder dusted our brows,
no longer were you among our number,
but our fighters were seething with bitter revenge,
and I saw it! Oh, I saw it: when the battle began,
all were emboldened by your strength and valor—
they were swift as deer and nimble as birds.

And it was your eyes sparking with fury
in each of their sweaty, raging faces . . .

Three days we carried you gathered in our arms,
in our gleaming eyes, pain and sorrow,
and every drop that dripped from your wound
fell on my heart like a bleeding ember.

Og
СЛЕЈ СЕ СО ТИШИНАТА (1955)

From

MERGE WITH THE SILENCE (1955)

УБАВИНАТА

На Л. Личеноски

Ме прогони како жена блудна,
ненаситна, похотна, осамена.
Ме грабнува во прегратка пламена
неизбежно и со сила судна.

И ме фрла со дланката лесна
в чудна игра, в чудно компонирање,
изгаснувам во грч и умирање
и се враќам в живот како песна.

Па со поглед што блика и зрачи,
потонувам до дно во модрината,
и кликнувам пак на убавината:
Прострелај ме со своите лачи!

Прострелај ме, па сè нека стивне
без расудок, без празно умување,
и блесокот на тоа лудување,
само твојот блесок нека вивне.

BEAUTY

To L. Ličenoski

It pursues me like a woman debauched,
insatiable, lonely, lecherous.
It seizes me in its fiery embrace
inescapably, with fateful force.

And lightly it tosses me into
a strange dance, a strange composition;
I dwindle away, die in convulsions,
and come back to life as a poem.

Then with a look, in a radiant cascade,
I drown in the depths of the blueness,
and call out again to the beauty:
Let me be pierced by your rays!

Pierce me that all may subside
without reasoning, without idle musing,
even the splendor of this madness—
so your splendor alone burns bright.

ВО ТИШИНА

Ако носиш нешто неизречено,
нешто што те притиска и пече,
закопај го во длабока тишина,
тишината сама ќе го рече.

IN SILENCE

If you carry a thing unspoken,
a thing that weighs on you and pains you,
bury it in deep silence;
the silence itself will speak it.

АХ ТАА УБАВИНА

Ах таа убавина, ах таа убавина,
тоа диво во крвта завивање.
Кине, граба, сече, носи како лавина,
вечна е притаеност и вечно откривање.

Не, не треба починка, не треба смирување,
сето поле пукнало од здравина,
па крвта е моја светло разденување
од таа разгаленост, од таа убавина.

OH THIS BEAUTY

Oh this beauty, oh this beauty,
this wild-in-the-blood howling—
it tears, grabs, cuts, carries me like an avalanche,
eternally hidden and eternally unveiling.

No—no need for rest, no need for calmness,
the entire field is bursting with health,
and in my blood a radiant dawning
from this extravagance, from this beauty.

КОГА ТИ Е НАЈТЕШКО

Кога ти е најтешко, кога ти се чини
дека гласот ти е крик, а погледот — молење,
загледај се, нурни се во водите сини,
ај, во таа свежина, во тоа шумолење.

Ќе сетиш со длабок здив
сила и смирување.
Погледот ќе блесне жив,
жив од подмладување.

WHEN TIMES ARE HARDEST

When times are hardest for you, when it seems
that your voice is a scream, your eyes, an appeal,
gaze into, dive into, waters of blue—
oh, into this freshness, this whispering.

Breathe deep and you will feel
strength and stillness growing.
Your eyes will light up, alive,
alive with youth renewing.

ГО БАРАМ СВОЈОТ ГЛАС

Го барам својот глас во молкот див на морето,
оно се скаменува.
Во жолтата пустина на есента го барам,
она зазеленува.
Моите раце не се мои раце
(моите раце се прсти на месечината).
Моите очи не се мои очи
(моите очи, очи за далечината).
Мојот збор е тврда вилица на времето
што 'рти по нивјето со заби на семето.

I SEEK MY VOICE

I seek my voice in the wild silence of the sea—
the sea turns to stone.
I seek it in the autumn's yellow desert—
the desert turns green.
My hands are not my hands
(my hands are fingers of moonlight).
My eyes are not my eyes
(my eyes are eyes for distance).
My word is the hard jawbone of time,
with teeth of seed that sprout in the fields.

ЛИСТ

Се откина од гранката сам, полека и несетено
и остана во воздухот да лебдее така.
Мислејќи дека е жолта пеперуга, детено
пружи по него рака.

И не се измени ни со прелив мал
на есента божилото.
Само гранката задржа скриена жал,
жал за зеленилото.

LEAF

It tore itself from the branch, slowly and unobserved,
and stayed there in the air, hovering.
Thinking it a yellow butterfly, the child
reached out her hand to grasp it.

And there was no change in the autumn rainbow,
not by the slightest hue.
Only the branch held on to its secret sorrow,
grieving for the green.

КОН ГАЛЕБОТ ШТО КРУЖИ НАД МОЈАТА ГЛАВА

Галебе мој,
не слетувај на моите очи.
На тие брегови откинати ниеден пристан нема.

Зарони во сите длабочини,
надлетај над сите височини
и дај виделина да земам!
Галебе мој, јас очи веќе немам.

Не слетувај на моето срце!
Галебе мој, срцето не е мое:
мини низ сите предели неминати,
крај сите живи, непознати, загинати.
Загледај во сите осамени, сите разделени,
и сите ледени врвои и сите ливади зелени,
и чуј —
додека твоето крило над нив морно се вие
како немирно во нив моето срце бие!

Не слетувај галебе мој,
врати се пак ва јатото.
Јас сум лотка, осудена
на судир со непознатото.

TO THE SEAGULL CIRCLING OVER MY HEAD

O my seagull,
do not alight upon my eyes.
These separated shores offer you no landing.

Plunge into all the depths,
soar above all the heights,
and bring me daylight—I will take it!
O my seagull, my eyes are vacant.

Do not alight upon my heart!
This heart, my seagull, is not mine:
Cross all the lands that have never been crossed,
past all the living, the unknown, the lost.
Look down at the lonely, at all who are divided,
at all the icy peaks and all the green meadows,
and listen—
as long as your wings beat wearily above them,
so will my heart beat restlessly within them.

Do not alight, my seagull,
but to your flock return.
I am a boat that is fated
to collide with the unknown.

ШТРК

Падна на ридот, еден штрк
сонува брегови зелени.
Му се привидува дека е пак
со јатата иселени.

Во летот долг се срушил он
и никој не го закрилува.
Seмне . . . и мисли дека е сон
првата снегулка што го милува.

STORK

Collapsed upon a hill, a stork
dreams of green shores.
He imagines he is back
with the migrating flock.

During the long flight he fell,
and no one caught him in their wings.
He shivers . . . and thinks it is a dream—
this first snowflake which caresses him.

ОБЛАК

Патник што нема ни пат ни цел
и со ветровите спие.
Од жед му напукнал образот бел
оган во очите крие.

Туѓ на секаков земен лик,
туѓ и на страстите свои.
Сам, како некој нестварен лик
меѓу луѓето и сонцето стои.

CLOUD

A traveler with neither path nor goal,
he sleeps among the winds.
His pure white cheeks are cracked with thirst,
his eyes are hiding fire.

Strange to every earthly shape,
to his own passions strange.
Alone, like a thing unformed,
between people and the sun.

НА ЕЗЕРО

Ледено спокојство. Езерска шир.
Тишина. Скаменет мир.

Само во висината,
во сончевината
две бели птици се капат.

Им бијат врело дамарите,
играат над шеварите
сѐ дури не потемне запад.

Наеднаш — немош и загинување . . .
Врз едно невидливо катче од езерото,
како непозната трпка врз телото,
помина бледо, лесно разбранување.
Водата сосема бавно се премрежи
и пак сѐ потона во камено смирување.

•

Кога ќе се разбранам и толку развилнеам
та да се кренам, да стигнам насекаде,
да давам секому сѐ што ветувам
и како далга неукротена
од брег на брег
моќно да прелетувам?

AT THE LAKE

Icy tranquility. A lake's expanse.
Silence. Frozen peace.

Only high above
two white birds
are bathing in the sunlight.

Blood beats hotly in their veins;
above the rushes they play
until the western sky darkens.

Suddenly—weakness and dwindling . . .
Across an invisible corner of the lake
a rippling rose up, faint and light
like an unknown tremor through the body.
The water was ever so slowly enlaced,
then everything settled again into stony calm.

•

When will I stir and well into rage,
so much that I rise, that I reach to every corner,
that I give to everyone all that I promise,
and like an untamed wave
from shore to shore
fly in all my strength?

ЛОВ НА ЕЗЕРО

Птица устремена. Стрвнина.
Исправен нор со закана.
Глуне езерска поврвнина,
модра од тага исплакана.

Темниот удар на крилото
темно ја сече модрината.
Блеснува на студенилото
рибата в клунот раскината.

Денот е сив од умирање.
Сами сме. Ништо не велиме.
Некое немо разбирање
нѐ гони да се разделиме.

HUNT ON THE LAKE

A bird, eyes fixed. Hunger.
A cormorant erect with threat.
Utterly still the lake's surface,
blue from sorrow wept.

The dark beat of the wings
darkly cleaves the blue.
In the bill the slashed fish
flashes in the cold.

The day is gray with dying.
We're alone. We don't say a word.
A certain mute understanding
is driving us apart.

ОБИЧНА УЛИЦА

Мојата улица нема куќи високи,
ни липи, ни маслини, ни багреми зелени.
Она понекогаш на мртво дрво личи
кај случајно ќе слетаат птиците иселени.

Мојата улица е мала и безимена,
со обични радости и обични грижи,
и да нема зеница од сонцето подгорена
не ќе може ништо со светот да ја зближи.

Низ мојата улица само јас поминувам
и само навечер штом се успие тишината
она се буди плашлива и измамена,
измамена од гласот на далечината.

AN ORDINARY STREET

There are no tall buildings on my street,
no lindens, no olives, no green locusts.
At times it seems like a withered tree,
where migratory birds alight by chance.

My street is small and has no name,
with ordinary joys and ordinary cares.
Were its eyes not scorched by the hot sun,
nothing could bring it close to the world.

No one but me walks down my street,
and at evening, once the silence is sleeping,
only then it awakes, alarmed and beguiled,
beguiled by the voice of the distance.

ЗАЛАЖУВАЊЕ

Таа ноќ е, сине, пеперуга бела:
на макова вршка слета и се скри.
Во маково цветје таа ноќ се вплела.
Не мисли ја ти.
Спи, сине, спи.

Таа ноќ е, сине, коњче што се спрема
да замине на пат неброени дни.
Сега сè е мирно. Сега ништо нема.
Смири се и ти.
Спи.

TRICKERY

The night, my son, is a white butterfly:
it alights on a poppy and there it hides,
nestled in the poppy flower soft and deep.
Put it out of your mind.
Sleep, my son, sleep.

The night, my son, is a horse getting ready
to leave on a journey long and steep.
Now all is calm. Now there is nothing.
You, too, settle down.
Sleep.

Од
ВЕТРОТ НОСИ УБАВО ВРЕМЕ
(1957)

From
THE WIND CARRIES
BEAUTIFUL WEATHER (1957)

БЕЛА ТАГА НА ИЗВОРОТ

Си отидов песно стара, песно невина,
си отидов без жалење.
За белата тага на изворот си отидов,
за непостојаната љубов на реките,
за грутка небо — од јаглен синевина,
за недостижните, за најдалеките.
Си отидов песно стара, песно невина,
си отидов без жалење.
А сега склупчена до прагот на утрината
една тешка неизвесност седи
и исто прашање без прекин повторува:
Зар вреди она што мислиш дека вреди?

Зашто знам —
сè ќе притивне кога дојде есента,
и реките ќе најдат љубов што смирува
кога ќе се сретнат со своите мориња,
и небото ќе узрее оплодено од песната
на житата, на лозјата, на маслините,
само белата тага на изворот
ќе остане иста, неизменета
како вечен копнеж за далечините.

THE WHITE SORROW OF THE SPRING

I left you, song of old, song of innocence,
left without regret.
For the white sorrow of the wellspring I left,
for the inconstant love of the rivers,
for a lump of sky the blueness of coal,
for the unreachable things, the most distant things.
I left you, song of old, song of innocence,
left without regret.
And now a weight of uncertainty sits
hunched on the doorstep of the morning,
repeating the same question over and over:
Is it really worth what you think it is worth?

Because I know:
everything will fall silent when autumn comes,
and when they join with the seas that are theirs,
the rivers will find a love that brings them peace,
and the sky will grow ripe, made fruitful by the song
of the grain and the vines and the olives.
Only the white sorrow of the spring will remain
the same as it was, unchanged—
like the eternal yearning for distances.

ЧУДАК

Тој не живее како останатите.
Со заматен поглед, очи устремени
оди по прагот на исчезнатите
со нова смисла да го обремени.

ODDBALL

He does not live as others do.
With clouded look, eyes riveted,
he walks the threshold of the lost
and with new meaning burdens it.

ЗДРАВИЦА

За вас ја кревам оваа чаша —
секому секој сам што сака
за вас и среќно, јас им велам,
а гледам кревам празна рака.

A TOAST

I raise this glass to you, my friends—
may each of you have the thing you want;
best of luck, I say to them,
and see myself raise an empty hand.

ДОБРА НОЌ

Вечерва умира нешто,
нешто што нема име.
Црно млеко некој пие од облаците,
а некој од право виме.

Добра ноќ.

GOOD NIGHT

Tonight something is dying,
something that has no name.
Someone is drinking black milk from the clouds,
another drinks from the udder.

Good night.

ИЛУЗИЈА

Ноќ. Во ноќта крлушки месечина.
Слева од планината безгласна далечина.

Сам во ноќта стасав до планината.
Еден свет е зад мене, една мака мината.

Глеј нешто во ветките шепоти притаено:
Сè што си присакувал сè е осознаено.

И овде, под планина, во оваа низина
дише далечината со дофатна близина.

Миг ... и сè исчезнува. Сон и пат. Далечина.
Сам сум. Над врвицата крлушки месечина.

ILLUSION

Night. In the night, scales of moonlight glisten.
From the mountain descends voiceless distance.

I have come here alone to the mountain at night.
Behind me a world, an anguish now past.

Listen—something whispers secretly in the wood:
All you have desired, all is understood.

And here beneath the mountain, down in this valley,
the distance is breathing so close I can feel it.

In an instant . . . all vanishes. Dream and pathway. Distance.
I am alone. Above the trail, scales of moonlight glisten.

КАЖИ МИ НЕБО

Кажи ми: Небо. Мое небо.
Кажи ми: Небо на тишината.
И јас, мало стебло во темната шума на крвта,
јас ќе се откорнам со сета вековна немоќ,
и извишен високо, високо, високо,
високо ко топла човечка зеница,
ќе станам небо, твое небо.
Ќе станам небо на една Деница.

Но, не кажувај ми дека сум слаб,
но не кажувај ми дека сум немоќен
и да им погледам в очи на тревките,
но не кажувај ми дека од сите треви
во мене шумат само најкревките.
Скриј ја и премолчи денес вистината
за едно мое поденешно утре.

Кажи ми: Небо. Мое небо.
Кажи ми: Небо на тишината.

CALL ME SKY

Call me—Sky. My sky.
Call me—Sky of the silence.
And I, a sapling in the dark forest of the blood,
will uproot myself and all this age-old weakness,
and rising high, high, high,
as high as a warm human eye,
will become sky—your sky.
I will become the sky of a Morning Star.

But do not say I am weak,
do not say I am not strong enough
even to look the grass in the eye,
do not say that of all the stalks of grass
only the most fragile hum inside me.
Keep it hidden and, today, hold back the truth
for an even more today tomorrow of mine.

Call me—Sky. My sky.
Call me—Sky of the silence.

БУДЕЊЕ

Пробуди се малечко. Зазорува. Зазорува.
Сонцето го испива изворот на сонот
и нешто неразумно кркори и зборува
со белото грло на ксилофонот.
Ах знам, зад портите 'ржат коњи впрегнати
што в лудечка љубов за срце те касаат,
пред нив се планините, покорно полегнати,
ни никогаш нигде они не ќе стасаат.
А овде е поле и мир на ливадите
и трева што 'рти во секоја жилка,
овде занесеноста на некогаш младите
никне како мала лековита билка.
Знам, сонот е среќа, и среќа и каење.
А овде горчината миг на едно траење.

Отвори ги очите. Погледај. Не чуди се.
Ден е. Ден. Пробуди се.

WAKING

Time to wake, little one. It is dawn. Dawn is breaking.
The sun is drinking up the source of your dream
and is burbling and chattering something inscrutable
through the white throat of the xylophone.
Oh, I know: beyond the gate harnessed horses are neighing,
and in their mad love they nip at your heart;
the mountains before them lie down in submission,
but these horses will never arrive anywhere.
And here is a field, and the meadow is peaceful,
and grass is growing in every vein;
here the exuberance of those who were young once
sprouts like a small healing herb from the ground.
I know: dreaming is joy—both joy and regret.
And bitterness here lasts only a moment.

Open your eyes. Look around. Do not be amazed.
It is daytime. Day. Time now to wake.

ТРЕБА ДА БИДЕМЕ ПОДОБРИ

Треба да бидеме подобри.
Треба да бидеме подобри.
Подобри од црвеното срце на лебот
од кој ни мириса сета соба
на Сонце, Земја и Глад.
Треба да бидеме подобри.
Треба да бидеме подобри.
Подобри од белите усни на водите
кои, љубејќи ги твоите колена,
шепотат за сите суводолици
и сите грла што сонуваат вино.
Треба да бидеме подобри.
Треба да бидеме подобри.
Подобри заради она дете
што го замислиле твоите утра
и божилото на твоето срце.
Заради оној добродушен човек
кој гледајќи те со „Добар ден"
смирено го зема својот обед.
Треба да бидеме подобри.
Треба да бидеме подобри.
Подобри од црвеното срце на лебот,
подобри од белите усни на водите,
заради нас,
заради нас,
заради човековиот „Добар ден",
заради она невино дете
што го замислиле твоите утра
и божилото на твоето срце.

WE HAVE TO BE BETTER

We have to be better.
We have to be better.
Better than the red heart of the bread
that fills the whole room with the aroma
of Sun and Earth and Hunger.
We have to be better.
We have to be better.
Better than the white lips of the water
that kiss your knees and speak in a whisper
of all the rivers that have run dry
and all the throats that are dreaming of wine.
We have to be better.
We have to be better.
Better for the sake of the child
who is imagined by your mornings
and by the rainbow in your heart.
Better for the sake of that kindly man
who wishes you "Good afternoon"
as he calmly enjoys his lunch.
We have to be better.
We have to be better.
Better than the red heart of the bread,
better than the white lips of the water,
for our own sake,
for our own sake,
for the sake of the man's "Good afternoon,"
for the sake of that innocent child,
who is imagined by your mornings
and by the rainbow in your heart.

ВЕТРОТ НОСИ УБАВО ВРЕМЕ

Ветрот носи убаво време.
Вилнее, јачи во нас.
Ветрот носи убаво време.

Убавото е убаво и поминува.
Останува тагата.
Понекогаш она нè обзема полека,
легнува на нашите очи,
и густо напластена
погледот ни го смрачува.
Тогаш нешто страшно тегобно и болно,
нешто големо и наше, непојмливо за другите
нè измачува.

Но некогаш тагата нè докоснува како трепетлика,
како измаглина премрежена над жуберлива река
крај која стоиме загледани бесцелно и немо.
Тогаш сите предмети прилегаат на сказна
па велиме: невозможно, колку е сè убаво.

Ветрот вилнее и јачи.
Ветрот носи убаво време.

THE WIND CARRIES BEAUTIFUL WEATHER

The wind carries beautiful weather.
It rages, it moans in us.
The wind carries beautiful weather.

The beautiful is beautiful and passes.
What remains is the sadness.
Sometimes it slowly engulfs us,
laying itself on our eyes
and thickly, layer upon layer,
darkening our view.
Then something torments us, terribly heavy and painful,
something large, and ours,
to others inconceivable.

Sometimes we are touched by the sadness like a quaking aspen,
like a lace of mist above a purling river,
which we stand beside staring out aimlessly, mutely.
Then all things have the look of a fairy tale,
and we say: it is all so impossibly beautiful.

The wind is raging and moaning.
The wind carries beautiful weather.

ПОДОЦНЕЖНИ ПЕСНИ

LATER POEMS

Од
ПЕСНА НА ЦРНАТА ЖЕНА
(1976)

From
THE SONG OF THE BLACK WOMAN
(1976)

БАОБАБ

Сето село го опколува не може да го опколи.
Дрво на животот. Храм на мртвите. Баобаб.
Сето село го опколува не може да го опколи.
Огронмно стебло. Куси гранки. Смирена молитва за дожд.
А дождовите ги нема.

Само една жена во модро, една црна жена во модро
застаната спроти стеблото
ги знае сите магии на дождот,
а никому не ги кажува.

Сонцето паѓа по утробата на земјата.
Земјата е сонце, сонцето е земја, сѐ ќе изгори од жед.
Само баобабот огромен им пркоси на горештините
смирен во молитва за дожд.
А дождовите ги нема.

Чиниш сега ќе се струполи, сушата во последниот дамар му чука.
Но наеднаш тој се исправа,
од корен се стресува,
магијата на жената во модро против природата го разбеснува.
Од своите сокови почнува да смука
и додека погледот му се разбиструва
разлистува, разлистува . . .
Зелен плач и молитва за дожд.
А дождовите ги нема.

Сето село го опколува не може да го опколи.
Дрво на животот. Храм на мртвите. Татковина.

THE BAOBAB

The entire village circling it cannot encompass it.
Tree of life. Temple to the dead. The baobab.
The entire village circling it cannot encompass it.
Giant trunk. Short branches. A quiet prayer for rain.
But the rains do not come.

A woman in blue, a black woman in blue,
stands opposite the tree—
she alone knows all the spells for rain,
but tells no one.

The sun is falling into the bowels of the earth.
Earth is sun, sun earth, and all will be consumed by thirst.
The giant baobab alone defies the heat,
quiet in its prayer for rain.
But the rains do not come.

Any moment, you think, it will crash down, drought knocking at its last vein,
when suddenly it stands erect,
trembling from its very root,
enraged against nature by the magic of the woman in blue.
It draws up its juices
and, its gaze growing brighter,
sprouts leaves, is sprouting one leaf after another . . .
Green weeping and a prayer for rain.
But the rains do not come.

The entire village circling it cannot encompass it.
Tree of life. Temple of the dead. Patrimony.

ВО СОНОТ НА ЦРНАТА ЖЕНА

Телото твое црна маслина,
најтемна бронза, најдлабок звук,
звук од там-тамите на твоите претци, од нивните старински кори.
По небото на твоето тело заорува невидлив плуг
и од црните бразди
секавично изгреваат сите потопени зори.

Телото твое неуморен ритам,
крвоток на океанот,
светлина темна што ме води по патека опасна и тесна,
од детство што ме прогони,
од порано, уште од утробата мајчина,
од првите зачетоци, најнесвесните.
Сега разбирам зошто не успеав да ти испеам ниедна песна
зашто самата си песна над песните.

Исплашен и страшен
стојам под небото на твоето тело
од твоите црни магии вџашен.
Ти ме разболуваш и ти ме лекуваш,
и ми велиш: јас сум твоја ноќ и твоја вечна луна,
биди спокоен, тука ќе векуваш,
мојот сон е пострашени од најстрашната буна.

Луно, црна луно,
од твоите магии вџашен
немам збор да ти противречи,
немам сила да ти се спротивстави.
Луно, црна буно,

INTO THE BLACK WOMAN'S DREAM

Your body, a black olive,
the darkest bronze, the deepest sound,
the sound of your ancestors' tom-toms, their ancient koras.
Across the sky of your body an invisible plow is pulled,
and all the sunken dawns
rise like lightning from the black furrows.

Your body, a tireless rhythm,
the bloodstream of the ocean,
a dark light that leads me down a narrow, dangerous path,
haunting me since childhood,
since before my childhood, from my mother's womb,
from my first, my most unconscious beginnings.
Now I understand why I could not sing a single song to you:
you are the song of songs.

Trembling and terrible,
I stand beneath the sky of your body,
bewildered by your black magic.
You wreck my health and make me well again,
you say to me: I am your night and your eternal moon.
Be calm, for here you will live long;
my dream is more terrible than the most terrible rebellion.

Moon, black moon,
stunned by your magic,
I have no word to contradict you,
I have no strength to oppose you.
Moon, black rebellion,

незарасната, неизлечена рано,
неусетно паѓам и тонам во твојот сон
како афричко сонце во океанот.

incurable, unhealed wound,
imperceptibly I fall, I sink into your dream,
like the African sun into the ocean.

ПРЕД РАСЦУТУВАЊЕ НА ФЛАНБОАЈАНИТЕ

Саноќ плачеше земјата
сува и испукана како препечена погача,
саноќ дуваа пустински ветрови
и трупаа песок во пукнатините.
Од преслекувања океанот ги испокина сите модри кошули,
а сепак не успеа да се смири.
Само небото остана спокојно и празно
како ништо да не се случува
како да не го гледа овој бродолом.

Саноќ урликаше земјата.
А можеби тоа беа жедните ѕверови
што лунѕаа низ саваните и шумите
умирајќи крај пресушените извори на вода.
А можеби тоа беа дрвјата што се свиваа до прекршување
и со лисјето ја лижеа сувата земја.
Само небото беше сурово спокојно и празно
како никому да не му е потребен дождот
како да не го гледа овој бродолом.

Саноќ се грчеше земјата.
А можеби тоа беа луѓето што го чекаа дождот
како што се чека првороденче
згрчено во безживотна утроба.
Пред изгрев сè се измори и се задрема таму кај што се најде
и луѓе и дрвја и ѕверови.
Врз океанот пливаа само парчиња од испокинатите кошули.
А со изгревот на сонцето како изгрев од раните

BEFORE THE FLAMBOYANTS BLOOMED

All night the earth was weeping,
dry and cracked like overbaked flatbread;
all night the desert winds were blowing,
filling the crevices with sand.
The ocean, changing its clothes, shredded its indigo garments,
but not even that could calm it.
Only the sky remained tranquil and empty,
as if nothing was happening,
as if it did not see this disaster.

All night the earth was howling.
Or maybe it was the thirsty animals
roaming the forests and savannas,
dying next to the dried-up springs.
Or maybe it was the trees bending to breaking point,
their leaves lapping at the arid earth.
Only the sky was cruelly tranquil and empty,
as if nobody needed the rain,
as if it did not see this disaster.

All night the earth was writhing.
Or maybe it was the people waiting for rain,
the way one waits for a first-born child
balled up in a lifeless womb.
Before dawn, everything dozed off, exhausted, right where it was,
people and trees and animals.
Only scraps of the shredded garments still floated on the ocean.
But with the rising of the sun

на земјата,
(црвени цветови и пожари, пожари во градот)
расцутеа фланбоајаните.

as if the wounds of the earth were rising
(red flowers and fires, fires in the city)
the flamboyants bloomed.

ЖЕНА ВО ИВЕРНАЖОТ

Се прелева чашата на ноќта. Истура пороен дожд.
Ноќ и дожд. Дожд и ноќ. Ивернаж.
И една жена сама во ноќта и ивернажот.
Под далечниот татнеж на там-тамите
змијулесто се извива на дождот
како во прегратка на маж.
Една жена во ноќната стара и чкрипава кола,
една жена од бучавата на дождот пробудена,
една жена од радост излудена
танцува во ноќта, на дождот, сама и гола.

А дожд врне како лекување на тешки рани,
како ослободување од темни сили и страсти,
врне како шепотење, како милување: Стани! Расти!
Дожд врне и нема крај на овој ивернаж,
додека жената змијулесто се извива на дождот
како во прегратка на маж.
Дожд врне и чудни приказни плете,
како раѓање и плач на првото дете.

WOMAN IN THE RAINY SEASON

The cup of the night overflows. Torrential rains pour down.
Night and rain. Rain and night. The *hivernage*.
And a woman alone in the night and the downpour.
She moves to the distant drumming of the tom-toms,
writhing snakelike in the rain
as if in the embrace of a man.
A woman in the old squeaky cart of the night,
a woman awakened by the roar of the rain,
a woman driven mad with joy,
dancing in the night in the rain, alone and naked.

And the rain comes down like healing for heavy wounds,
like freedom from dark forces and passions,
it comes down like murmurings, like caresses: Arise! Grow!
The rain comes down and this *hivernage* will never end
so long as the woman dances snakelike in the rain,
writhing as if in the embrace of a man.
The rain comes down and weaves its strange tales,
like the birth and the wail of your first-born child.

НАСТАН НА ЕЗЕРСКИОТ БРЕГ

Веста прелета секавично
и сиот народ слезе на езерскиот брег
каде тој лежеше преморен и забревтан од долгиот пат,
тој крилест коњ со ѕвездена светлина во очите,
со сибирско иње во ноздрите,
со сахарска песочна прав во гривата.
Сиот свет го обиколи, ги прелета сите мориња и океани
и одвај смогна сили да се спушти тука на родното езеро
за да се напие бистра вода, ладна и лековита.
Слета и легна на брегот, забревтан од долгото патување,
легна крај езерото, а немаше сили да го направи
последниот напор: да се нурне во водата бистра и лековита
што ќе му ги собере силите
и ќе му го поврати животот.
Собраниот народ се туркаше и мрмореше крај него:
жените му се молеа на бога милозливо, децата цараа со очите
за едни од мажите тоа беше невидена лудост,
за други попусто патување и бесцелен летот,
додека за него тоа беше највисока смисла на животот
да ја открие родината откривајќи го светот.
Три дни лежеше тој крај водата езерска
без сили да се созeме,
три дни ни стануваше ни умираше.
Три дни народот чекаше трпеливо,
а четвртиот ден почна полека да се прибира дома
оставајќи го сам коњот на езерото.
И токму последниот човек тргна да си оди
кога плисна пороен дожд и езерото почна да нараснува
а бранови да го заплискуваат коњот крај езерото.
Од бистрата вода и лековита созeмен

AN EVENT BY THE LAKE

The news spread like lightning
and all the people descended on the lakeshore,
where he lay exhausted and winded from his long journey—
the winged horse with starlight in his eyes,
Siberian hoarfrost in his nostrils,
the dust of the Saharan sand in his mane.
He had circled the world, crossed all seas and oceans,
and barely found the strength to alight here, by his native lake,
that he might drink its clear, cool, and health-giving water.
He flew down and lay on the shore, winded from his long travels;
he lay down next to the lake but lacked the strength to make
one final effort—to plunge into the clear and health-giving water
that would restore his strength to him,
that would return his life to him.
The people were gathered around him, jostling and murmuring,
the women praying to God for mercy, the children gawking.
For some of the men, this was inconceivable madness,
for others, a journey in vain, a pointless flight,
but for him, it was the highest purpose of his life:
to discover his native land by discovering the world.
Three days he lay by the water of the lake
without the strength to revive himself.
Three days he neither recovered nor died.
Three days the people waited with patience,
but on the fourth day they slowly began to make their way home,
leaving the horse alone by the lake.
And just as the last person was getting ready to leave,
the rain came down in torrents and the lake began to rise
and its waves began to lap against the horse beside the lake.
Revived by the clear and health-giving water,

коњот 'рзна неколку пати колку што грлото можеше да го додржи,
а народот исплашен почна да се враќа назад
и без да сака го виде коњот како се нурка во езерото
како се игра со брановите и пие вода бистра и лековита.
Сево ова траеше само неколку мига,
а потоа коњот излезе на брегот
и повторно се вивна нагоре како првпат да го започнува летот,
носејќи ја со себе својата највисока смисла
откривајќи ја родината да го открие светот.

the horse neighed a few times, as much as his throat could manage,
and the startled people began to return;
they could not take their eyes away as the horse plunged into the lake,
as he frolicked with the waves and drank the clear and health-giving
    water.
It lasted just a few moments,
and then the horse came out onto the shore
and lifted himself again into the air, as if this were his very first flight,
carrying with him his highest purpose:
to discover his native land and so discover the world.

ЗАГЛЕДАН ВО ОКЕАНОТ

Еден човек загледан во океанот,
еден човек загледан во брановите на океанот,
стои долго неподвижен на брегот
небаре ја прелистува судбата на својот народ.
Човекот не забележува дека времето одминува,
дека веќе одамна не е пладне,
дека сонцето скока по водените нерамнини
како огромен ранет црвен галеб,
и дека уште малку само па ќе се спушти насекаде
бескрајна афричка ноќ.

Човекот неподвижно стои како скаменета жал.
Океанот е огромен, а човекот мал.

Еден мал човек загледан во брановите на океанот
стои на брегот и во мислите ги довикува
сите галии на своите непознати претци
испловени пред многу векови
на пат кон неизвесното и непознато Утре.
Човекот стои и не забележува
дека веќе се прекрили бескрајната афричка ноќ
и дека е сè завиено со едно црно и огромно Ништо —
и земја и небо и вода.
Човекот стои и упорно и понатаму гледа.
Наеднаш огромното црно Ништо како да се раздвижува,
како да оживува.
Од неговите длабини изронуваат
сите дамна испловени галии,
сите младичи и девојки одведени или потопени пред многу векови,
и полека, но сигурно веслаат и се приближуваат коњ брегот

GAZING AT THE OCEAN

A solitary man gazing at the ocean,
a solitary man gazing at the waves of the ocean,
stands motionless a long time on the shore
as if perusing the fate of his people.
The man does not notice that time is passing,
that noon was long ago,
that the sun is skipping across the ripples of the water
like an immense wounded red gull,
and that soon everywhere
an endless African night will descend.

The man stands motionless like a pillar of sorrow.
The ocean is immense; the man, small.

A small solitary man gazing at the waves of the ocean
stands on the shore and in his thoughts is calling
to all the galleys of his unknown ancestors
who sailed away on a journey centuries ago
to an uncertain, unknown Tomorrow.
The man stands there and does not notice
that the endless African night has already folded itself in its wings,
and all is wrapped in immense black Nothingness—
land and sky and water.
The man stands there tirelessly peering even further into the distance.
All at once the immense black Nothingness seems to move,
seems to be coming to life.
Emerging from its depths
are all the galleys that sailed away long ago,
all the young men and women carried off or drowned centuries ago,
and slowly but surely they are approaching, rowing to the shore,

чија граница не се ни назира во мракот.
Но човекот на брегот ги насетува,
долго им мавта со раце,
ги довикува,
надвикувајќи се со страшниот глас на океанот.
И еве — тие наидуваат,
веќе се искрцуваат на брегот
носејќи ја на раце својата тешка и недоречена судба,
својата ненапишана историја.
Човекот на брегот скока од радост,
со сите се гушка, со сите се љуби
и незабележано исчезнува, се губи меѓу нив.
Човекот се слева со огромната маса,
огромната маса со човекот.

. . . .

Одамна веќе и ноќта помина,
сонцето повторно избива над брегот на океанот
сцрвенето од радост и жал.

А човекот упорно стои и гледа во брановите на океанот.
Човекот е огромен, океанот мал.

whose limit cannot be seen in the darkness.
But the man on the shore senses them
and for a long time is waving at them,
calling to them,
shouting above the ocean's terrible voice.
And here they are—arriving,
already disembarking on the shore,
carrying in their hands their heavy fate, never fully told,
their unwritten history.
The man on the shore is leaping for joy,
hugging them all, kissing them all,
until he unnoticeably disappears, is lost among them.
The man merges with the immense mass,
the immense mass merges with the man.

. . . .

Night has long since passed;
above the ocean shore the sun is rising again,
ruddied with joy and sorrow.

But tirelessly the man stands watching the waves of the ocean.
The man is immense; the ocean, small.

СВЕТЛИНАТА НА РОБОВИТЕ

тука ме доведе моето провидение

Оставете ме тука добри мои црни пријатели
и да го барав немаше да го пронајдам ова место
што го открив случајно.
Тука ме доведе мојата исконска страст
за трагање низ мрачните но неизбежни свијоци на историјата
мојата вечна жед за изворите на сеопштото потекло
и гладта моја за невеселата младост на човештвото.
Тука ме доведе мојот прародителски инстинкт
и неговиот непогрешлив шепот дека сè е исто
иако е сокриено во различни шуми и растенија
без оглед како и да се викаат: баобаб, даб или бреза.

Околу баобабот сите села на еден народ се собираат,
го опколуваат, но не можат да го опколат,
затоа што внатре во стеблото, закопани исправено, лежат мртвите
и водат таен духовен разговор со своите потомци,
а мртвите никој не успеал да ги опколи;
околу дабот бршлени млади се извиваат и танцуваат
и од своите сокови со вечна младост го опијануваат,
а соковите на бршлените никој не успеал да ги пресекне;
а околу брезата девојки — красавици како сињарки од север
раскажуваат приказни за љубовта, широка како нивната земја
и длабока како нивната душа,
а приказните за љубовта никој не успеа да ги дослуша.

THE LIGHT OF THE SLAVES

here my providence has led me

Leave me here, my good black friends—
even if I had been looking for it, I would not have found this place
which I discovered by accident.
I was led here by my primordial passion for searching
the dark twists of history,
by my eternal thirst for the sources of our universal ancestry
and by my hunger for the unhappy youth of humanity.
I was led here by my atavistic instinct
and its unmistakable whisper telling me that everything is the same,
although hidden in different forests and plants,
regardless of what they are called: baobab, oak, or birch.

Around the baobab gather all the villages of a people;
they circle it but cannot encompass it,
because buried upright in its trunk are the dead, conducting
a secret spiritual conversation with their descendants,
and no one has yet managed to encompass the dead.
Around the oak, young ivy twines and dances,
and its juices intoxicate the tree with eternal youth,
and no one has yet managed to dry up the juices of the ivy.
And around the birch, beautiful girls, like northern Signares,
tell stories of a love as wide as their land
and as deep as their soul,
and no one has yet managed to hear love stories to the end.

Оставете ме тука добри мои пријатели,
тука ме повика исконската страст
да ја пронајдам својата праслика
изгубена во мрачните свијоци на времето,
но жива и силна како вдахновение.
Оставете ме, оставете ме тука. Тука ме доведе моето провидение.

загледани во сонцето

Јас — кој роб бев,
и ти — што беше роб, а сега си камен,
сега си Куќа на робовите
што се извишува како закана, како светилник над островот
сто милиони пати посилен од светилникот на Мамел
што им го осветлува патот на авионите и бродовите —
тие сегашни гусари на модерната цивилизација —
што сакаат да го ограбат небото и водите на океанот.

Твојата светлина доаѓа од длабочината на вековите,
од ниските сламени колиби во саваните и прашумите
каде што седиш со својата жена и деца
и сите толчете пченка за да испечете леб,
а никој не се ни праша што со лебот и дали ќе ви стаса.
Вам ви е доволно да гледате во сонцето што заоѓа
како се вплеткува меѓу гранките и се обесува на најтенката,
па личи, страшно личи на закрвавено око
што само вас ве гледа, а ти им велиш на децата:
„Тоа е окото на нашиот Голем Татко, неговите солзи
што ги собирал додека одел по земја,
како светлина ќе ги прострелаат тревите и дрвјата,
и сè ќе се исплаши и ќе замре: и птици и диви животни
и змии цицачи и отровни гуштери,

Leave me here, my good friends;
here my primordial passion has summoned me
to discover my archetype,
which is lost in the dark twists of time
but alive and strong as inspiration.
Leave me, leave me here. Here my providence has led me.

gazing at the sun

I—who was a slave—
and you—who were a slave but are now a stone,
are now a House of Slaves
that towers like a threat, like a lighthouse over the island,
a hundred million times brighter than the Lighthouse of the Mamelles,
which lights the way for planes and ships,
those latter-day pirates of modern civilization,
that seek to plunder the sky and the ocean waters.

Your light comes from the depths of the ages,
from the low straw huts in the savannas and ancient forests
where you sit with your wife and children,
and all of you thresh corn to bake your bread,
and no one even asks about the bread and whether it will suffice.
It is enough for you to look at the setting sun
as it weaves itself into the branches and hangs upon the thinnest of them,
so it resembles—frighteningly resembles—a bloodshot eye
that looks only at you and your family, and you tell the children:
"That is the eye of our Great Father, and the tears
that welled in him as he walked the earth
will pierce the grass and trees as light,
and all will be afraid and stop dead in their tracks: birds and wild animals,
snakes, mammals and poisonous lizards,

и наеднаш ќе падне бескрајна глува ноќ над Африка
штом окото-сонце ќе се струполи во океанот“.
А кога завладее глува ноќ над Африка
ти се чини дека никогаш не си видел виделина.

Децата се припиваат до мајка си,
а заедно со неа сите до тебе.
А ти за да ги смириш долго им раскажуваш
за добрите духови, за прародителите,
за нивната среќа смрт што починале на својата земја,
зашто само така се одржува врската со живите.
Со секоја твоја нова приказна очите на децата сè повеќе се распалуваат
отпрвин налик на мали пламени што како јазици
го лижат работ на шумите
но силниот ветар на приказните ги разгорува
и во очите избувнува страшен пожар
што се заканува сè да изгори во шумите.
Очите на децата набргу почнуваат да прилегаат
на окото-сонце на Големиот Татко,
и нивниот пламен дури тука допира
тука на Горе — до Куќата на робовите.

Припиен за неа како камен се одронувам
и во таа светлина потонувам, потонувам.

со приокован поглед во црна Африка

Овие бигори океанот ги исфрлил на брегот,
ги исфрлил овде на островот од каде што некогаш,
стројни и лични младичи и девојки со прикован проштален поглед
во својата родна Црна Африка,
со галии ги испраќале како живо црно робје во туѓи континенти.

and an endless deep night will fall suddenly over Africa
when the sun-eye plunges into the ocean."
And when deep night reigns over Africa
you will think you had never seen daylight.

The children huddle close to their mother,
and they all huddle close to you.
And to calm them, you tell them stories
about the good spirits, about the ancestors,
whose good fortune it was to have died in their own country,
for this is the only way to preserve the connection with the living.
With each new story the eyes of the children blaze even more,
resembling at first little flames that lap like tongues
at the edges of the forest,
but the strong wind of the stories fuels these flames
and a terrible fire flares in the children's eyes,
threatening to burn everything in the forest.
Soon the eyes of the children begin to resemble
the sun-eye of the Great Father,
and their flames reach even here,
here to the island of Gorée—to the House of the Slaves.

Huddled against it, I am crumbling like a stone
and sinking, sinking, into this light.

with eyes fixed on Africa

These heavy stones the ocean has tossed onto the shore,
tossed here onto this island from where
handsome young men and women, their eyes fixed in a farewell gaze
on their own native Africa,
were once sent in galleys as living black slaves to foreign continents.

Океанот им станувал и дом и безмилосна судбина,
додека одвај во далечина се насирала непознатата земја
што им ветувала денови поцрни од нивната кожа.
Непознатата земја останала туѓа и непозната,
а жалта за родниот брус ги збигорувала нивните души
што се откорнувале од телата. Исушените тела
лежеле како празни рибји костури на туѓата земја,
а збигорените души остри и иглести се тркалале до океанот.
Безмилосниот океан ги пречекувал како најзагрижен родител,
ги прегрнувал со своите раце-бранови и ги носел назад,
назад кон Горе од каде што некогаш
како стројни младичи и девојки ги испраќале со галии
во непознати и далечни туѓи континенти,
а сега се бигори исфрлени на брегот,
со вечно прикован поглед во својата Црна Африка,
сега се Куќа на робовите
во нем и присен допир со потомците
да си поприкажуваат и да починат.

моќта на там-тамот

Темно е небото, темен е и океанот,
а најтемна е земјата.
Сè се засолнило в глувото дувло на темнината.
Но звукот на там-тамот со светлосен куршум ја преполовува
и двете половини крвавеат ко румени усни на зората.
Там-тамот е мистериозна тајна на животот,
од најдлабок сон живите ги скорива,
мртвите ги враќа во танец со живите,
а робовите излегуваат од своите бигори
и го живеат својот предвреме прекинат живот.
Там-тамот ги опијанува сите како палмино вино,

The ocean became both their home and their merciless fate,
as faintly in the distance an unknown land began to appear,
a land that promised them days blacker than their skin.
The unknown land would remain to them foreign and unknown,
while longing for their native wilds calcified their souls,
which tore themselves from their bodies. The dried-up bodies
lay on the foreign land like empty fish skeletons,
while the calcified souls, sharp and needle-like, rolled down to the ocean.
The merciless ocean was waiting for them like a most anxious parent;
it embraced them in its wave-arms and carried them back,
back to Gorée, from where, as handsome young men and women,
they had once been sent in galleys
to unknown and distant foreign continents,
and now they are stones tossed onto the shore,
with eyes fixed eternally on their Africa;
now they are a House of Slaves
in silent and intimate contact with their descendants,
to converse with them for a time and then rest.

the power of the tom-tom

The sky is dark, and dark the ocean,
but darkest of all is the land.
Everything takes cover in the deep recesses of the darkness.
But the sound of the tom-tom severs the gloom with a blast of light,
and its two halves bleed like the red lips of the dawn.
The tom-tom is a mysterious sacrament of life;
it wakes the living from the deepest dreams,
it brings back the dead to dance with the living,
and the slaves emerge from their heavy stones
to resume their lives, so early interrupted.
The tom-tom intoxicates everyone like palm wine,

и сè е замелушено: и природа и човек и вода и растение,
там-тамот е празник и славје на животот,
там-тамот е општо воскресение.

Грмне ли там-тамот ден се разденува,
сите срипуваат на нозе од својата незадржлива крв прогонети
живи и мртви, болни и неизлечени,
танецот се извива низ селата, низ саваните,
покрај реките, низ прашумите,
и како бескраен ритам и мелодија
се извишува нагоре, нагоре до сонцето
каде што од крошните на џиновските дрвје
насмевнат гледа Големиот Татко.

А Куќата на робовите станува раскошен дворец и борилиште
низ кое достоинствено чекорат некогашните робови,
и облечени како принцовите од Мали
се борат за срцето на своите избрани сињарки.

во очите на сињарките

Оставете ме тука добри мои пријатели,
и да го барав немаше да го пронајдам ова место
случајно што го открив.
Оставете ме тука меѓу овие бигори
со уште еден бигор да ја извишам Куќата на робовите.
Звукот на там-тамот да ме пренесува преку реките Гамбија и Конго,
а горе преку Нигер до земјата на Догоните;
младите сињарки со песни да ме успиваат
и успан да ја сонувам младоста непоминлива.
Во сините очи на црноликите сињарки
да изгрева синилото на мојата татковина.

and all are confounded: nature and man and water and plants;
the tom-tom is a holiday and festival of life,
the tom-tom is universal resurrection.

The tom-tom thunders and a new day dawns;
everyone leaps to their feet, impelled by their irrepressible blood—
living and dead, sick and incurable—
and the dance weaves through the villages, through the savannas,
along the rivers, through the jungles,
and rises as an endless rhythm and melody
upwards, upwards, to the sun,
where from the tops of gigantic trees
the Great Father watches with a smile.

And the House of Slaves becomes a luxurious palace and arena,
where the former slaves now stride in majesty,
and, arrayed like princes of Mali,
they compete for the heart of their chosen Signare.

in the eyes of the Signares

Leave me here, my good friends—
even if I had been looking for it, I would not have found this place
which by accident I discovered.
Leave me here among these heavy stones,
that I may make the House of Slaves one more stone higher.
That the sound of the tom-tom may carry me across the Gambia and
    Congo Rivers,
and up across the Niger to the Land of the Dogons;
that the young Signares may lull me to sleep with their songs,
and that, sleeping, I may dream of a never-passing youth.
That in the blue eyes of the dark-cheeked Signares
the blue sky of my homeland may rise.

А кога там-тамот ќе го домами ивернажот
песната на дождовите да биде песна на сеопшто раѓање.
А јас — бигор искачен на Куќата на робовите
и замаен од вишините,
да се нурнам со таа песна и да исчезнам во убавините.

And that, when the tom-tom lures out the *hivernage,*
the song of the rains may be a song of universal birth.
And that I—a stone lifted onto the House of Slaves
and dizzy from the height—
may dive with this song and disappear into the beauty.

Од
ДРВО НА РИДОТ (1980)

From

THE TREE ON THE HILL (1980)

ДОМОТ НА СОНОТ

Ме осудивте да седам дома, добри мои пријатели,
затворен во својата темна несреќа
да не излегувам во рани зори кога мугрите пукаат како црвени
	трендафили
и сето небо го облева огромна пламната жар.
Нека, ме осудивте да седам дома и јас ќе седам додека можам
и ќе ги довикувам тие црвени трендафили, таа жар
да ги ожари сите утроби ладни, сите за црвени соништа гладни.

Ме осудивте да седам дома и јас смирено ќе седам.
Но каде е домот на сонот? Кој ли ќе му забрани на сонот
да не се извишува повисоко од зорите,
поитро од развигорите,
и кога ќе се измори кој ли ќе му забрани да не се успие
со најцрвените, со најмилите
од трендафилите?

THE HOME OF THE DREAM

You have condemned me to sit at home, my good friends,
locked in my dark misfortune,
to not go out in the morning light, when dawns are exploding like red
    roses
and the whole sky is washed in the glow of flaming embers.
So be it. You have condemned me to sit at home and I will sit here as long
    as I can;
I will call on those red roses, on those embers,
to inflame all whose bowels are cold, all who hunger for red dreams.

You have condemned me to sit at home and I will sit here peacefully.
But where is home for the dream? Who will forbid the dream
to ascend higher than the morning light,
more nimbly than the soft spring breezes?
And when it wears itself out, who will forbid it to sleep
with the reddest, the dearest
of roses?

СЕДАМ САМ СО СВОЈОТ ПЛАМЕН ВО ГРАДИТЕ

Седам сам, заробен во зелената одаја на дворот.
Нема никого: ни пријатели, ни блиски, ни непознати.
Сѐ е смирено. Само тишината ги дебне и ги лови
немирните шумови на лисјето и веднаш ги скаменува.

Ноќта се отвора благородно како цвет што разденува.
Пука некоја невидлива пупка на црвен трендафил
и од пукнатите лисје ѕирка пожар со црвено лице.
Пупката расте, се шири и сиот двор го ожарува,
но за миг црвениот трендафил исчезнува и пожарот згаснува.
А црвениот пламен го бара местото на моето срце
и таму полека во огромно пламено дрво израснува.

Седам сам, заробен во зелената одаја на дворот.
Нема никого: ни пријатели, ни блиски, ни непознати.

Седам сам со својот пламен во градите.
Пламенот ме огрева посилно и од зборот на поетите
исчезнати во свемирот и синевината
барајќи го светот на убавината,
непозната и ненадмината.

Црвениот трендафил како крв се шири, истекува
а овој пламен во градите навек тука ќе векува.

I SIT ALONE WITH MY FLAME IN MY BREAST

I sit alone, imprisoned in the green room of the yard.
No one is here—not friends, not loved ones, not strangers.
Everything is calm now. Only silence lies in wait, to catch
the restless murmurs of the leaves, which it instantly turns to stone.

The night opens nobly, like a flower unfurling the day.
The bud of a red rose, unseen, is breaking
and from its cracked leaves a red-faced fire peeps out.
The bud grows, expands, and sets the entire yard ablaze,
but a moment later the red rose vanishes and the fire dies away.
The red flame finds a place in my heart,
and there it slowly grows into a great flaming tree.

I sit alone, imprisoned in the green room of the yard.
No one is here—not friends, not loved ones, not strangers.

I sit alone with my flame in my breast.
It warms me more intensely than even the words of the poets
who vanished in the cosmos and the blueness,
searching for the world of beauty,
of a beauty unknown and unsurpassed.

The red rose, like blood, is spreading, spilling out,
and this flame in my breast will remain here forever.

ОД НАЈСТАРА И НАЈЧИСТА СОНЧЕВИНА

Од тешка болест телото ми е закоравено
и на врв планина само да чамее оставено.
Ту тешки магли и непрозирни го натрупуваат
и видот со сиот свет му го засолнуваат.
Ту дождови го бијат ко ситни острици новородени
и плуштат по телото ко удари неоплодени.

Но наеднаш маглите се губат и разредуваат
и дождовните ситни капки исчезнуваат.
Сонцето се раѓа во земјата на својот Изгрев
и пристига до земјите на својот Залез.
Лицето му е чисто и измиено
од најситната прашинка во семирот сокриено.

А телото мое закоравено
се раздвижува заздравено
и пие од сонцето вина
од најстара и најчиста сончевина.

OF THE OLDEST AND PUREST SUNLIGHT

My body has grown stiff with heavy sickness
and is left alone on a mountaintop to languish.
Heavy, impermeable fogs now pile around it,
its view of the whole world obliterating.
Now rains beat down like tiny sharp blades newborn,
pummeling at my body like fists forlorn.

But all at once the fogs are lifting, melting;
the tiny raindrops are evaporating.
The sun is being born in the land of its Rising,
and in the lands of its Setting, is arriving.
Pure and cleansed is its countenance,
hidden from the tiniest dust in the cosmos.

And my body, grown stiff,
is limber and healthy again,
and drinks the wine of the sun,
of the oldest and purest sunlight.

СОНЦЕТО И ТЕЛОТО

Од својот Изгрев до својот Залез
страотен пат сонцето изодува — низ магли, низ сончеви ветришта,
    низ пепелишта.
И кога ја надвишува планината забележува како чамее осамено
телото мое заборавено.
Сонцето се ведне и запира и на телото му вели:
„Тргај со мене, време немаме, треба на пат да одиме".
Телото го открива гласот на жена си и со крик ѝ вели:
„Во живот низ смрт, мила моја, води ме!"
Сонцето се извишува нагоре, со лице надолу виснато,
а телото останува на планина од тешка болест притиснато.
Но утредента сето тоа пак се повторува, и задутре пак.
И секој ден сонцето почнува од Земјата на својот Изгрев
до Земјите на својот Залез,
каде одеднаш пропаѓа во океанот на океаните
да си ги разлади раните.

Но еден прекрасен ден кога го повика телото
и се извиши, не забележа како со него лета во вишината
и телото, што пие вина од Сончевината.

THE SUN AND THE BODY

From its Rising to its Setting
the sun travels a terrifying path—through fog, through solar winds,
    through ash.
And as it rises over the mountain, it spies my body languishing alone,
my forgotten body.
The sun, stopping, bends down and says to the body:
"Come with me—we have no time, we must be on our way."
The body recognizes the voice of its wife and, with a cry, says to her:
"Lead me, my dear one, through death into life!"
The sun climbs higher, its face looking down,
but the body remains on the mountain, weighed down by heavy illness.
The next day the same thing happens again, and again the day after.
And every day the sun starts out from the land of its Rising
and travels to the lands of its Setting,
where it drops suddenly into the ocean of oceans
to cool its wounds.

But one fine day as it calls out to the body
and then climbs higher, it does not see that behind it in the heights
the body, too, is flying, drinking the wine of the Sunlight.

ГНЕЗДО ВО БРАНОВИТЕ

Една птица од топлите јужни краишта,
изморена од долго летање и замелушена од врела сончевина,
споулавено кружи над езерото и во чаталестото дрво
разлистено над воденото огледало
го бара своето скриено старо гнездо
каде единствено може да отпочине и да се смири.

Лета птицата, одвај кружи и дрвото не го препознава.
Дрвото се подмладило, разгранило и чиниш го прекрило сето езеро.
Илјади други птици ноќевале во неговите крошни
и исчезнувале со раните утрински шумови.
А оваа птица секоја година долетувала,
слетувала во своето гнездо и не забележувала
како со времето ја издаваат силите
и како веќе не е онаа истата што може
неуморно да лета и да се опијанува
од чистиот воздух и од опојниот мирис на дрвото.

Долго кружи оваа споулавена птица над водата,
над огромните разлистени гранки на дрвото
под кои се набира езерото премрежено
од ветрот што носи оддалеку сè посилни бранови.
Грбавите бранови ѝ заличуваат на птицата
на нејзиното старо добро легло свиено во дрвото
и таа со последни сили се стрмоглавува кон своето гнездо,
со страшен свиреж на воздухот мине низ гранките
и без крик удира и исчезнува во брановите.

A NEST IN THE WAVES

A bird from the warm southern regions,
exhausted from long flying and dazed by the blistering sun,
circles frantically above the lake, searching a wide-branching tree
that overhangs the watery mirror,
trying to find her own, old, hidden nest,
the only place she can rest and calm herself.

The bird is flying, barely circling, and does not recognize the tree.
The tree has gained new life, put out new branches, and seems to cover
    the entire lake.
Thousands of other birds have spent the night in its crown,
disappearing with the hum of early morning.
But this bird has flown here year after year,
flying down into her nest and not noticing
that over time her strength has been failing her,
and that she is no longer the same bird able
to fly without tiring and be drunk
on the pure air and the tree's heady scent.

Long does this frantic bird circle above the water,
above the huge, leafy branches of the tree,
beneath which the lake is rising, roiled
by the wind, which brings from afar ever more powerful waves.
To the bird, the hump-shaped waves resemble
the fine old bed she had woven in the tree,
and so with her last strength she dives headlong towards her nest;
with a terrible whistling sound she passes through the branches,
strikes the surface without a cry and disappears into the waves.

Дрвото вчудоневидено ги развива гранките
над разбеснетото езеро
како да сака да ја гушне птицата
што сиот свој живот го мина во своето гнездо,
а сега исчезна во гнездото на брановите
каде единствено може да отпочине и да се смири.

The tree, stunned, unfolds its branches
above the furious lake,
as if wanting to embrace the bird
that has spent her entire life in her nest
but now has disappeared into the nest of the waves,
the only place she could rest and calm herself.

ДРВО НА РИДОТ

Од дамни дамнини расте ова дрво на сува рида без вода
со гранки раскрилени ко птица далдисана во летот.
Високото сонце го заслепува од својот усвитен светлосен одар,
но во него шуркаат сите живи сокови на светот.

И лете му шумолат гранките
и зиме кога заснежува,
а светот го забележува и не го забележува.

Ветришта диви го сардисуваат и сеништа темни,
тврдата почва и испукана бистриот поглед му го засенува,
суши змијарници му ги смукаат корењата земни,
но тоа од пркос зазеленува и расте, расте и зазеленува.

Љубов моја, те сретнав на овој рид како патник во мугри што
        подранува
ти дадов сè што можам, а сè било јаловина.
Под дрвото се љубевме и израснавме, сушата ни беше ладовина,
сега ние си одиме, а дрвото опстојува и останува.

Дај, господи, исполни ми ја последната желба
при оваа голема делба —
да се најдеме и слееме со срцевината
на ова дрво што расте на сува рида во вишината.

THE TREE ON THE HILL

For a long, long time this tree has grown on an arid hill without water,
its branches spread wide like a bird absorbed in flight.
The high sun from its hot, blazing dais dazzles it blind,
yet all the life juices of the world are surging inside it.

The rustling of its branches is heard in the summer,
and even in the winter, when it is snowing,
and the world both notices and takes no notice.

Wild gusts of wind besiege it, and dark ghosts, too,
the hard, cracked soil turns its bright gaze dim,
droughts like snake pits suck at its earth-bound roots,
but still it is proudly green and grows, it grows and is green.

My love, I met you on this hill like a traveler who rises at dawn.
I gave you all that I could, but all of it was barrenness.
Beneath this tree we loved each other and grew older—drought to us was
     coolness—
and now we are leaving, but the tree endures and remains.

May God grant me one last wish
at this great parting of ways—
that we find each other again and join as one with the core
of this tree that grows on an arid hill high into the air.

ДОДАТОК

АЦО ШОПОВ ЗА СКОПСКИОТ ЗЕМЈОТРЕС ВО 1963 ГОДИНА

APPENDIX

ACO ŠOPOV ON THE SKOPJE EARTHQUAKE OF 1963

ВО ПЕТ И СЕДУМНАЕСЕТ

Некој запиша: на дваесет и шести јули илјада деветстотини шеесет и трета, во пет и седумнаесет, загина градот на Вардар.

Каква страотна пресуда на природата, каква катастрофална закана на вистината, содржана во еден единствен миг од времето – пет и седумнаесет. Во ревот на земјата и бетонските блокови – пет и седумнаесет. Во вителот на зданијата и стемнетото сонце – пет и седумнаесет. Во крикот на децата чиј што сон ни под урнатините не успеа да избега од зелените поља на нивните очи – пет и седумнаесет. Во дивата занеменост на мајките и татковците, на младичите и девојките, на човекот кој во еден единствен миг остана гол врз пепелот на разорените зданија и врз кого се сруши нечовечки товар од бол и патила – пет и седумаесет.

Пет и седумнаесет. Кој би можел со нашите обични човечки зборови да ја искаже драмата во која слепата утроба на земјата вовлече двеста иљади жители на оваа планета, драмата Пет и седумнаесет.

Да, изгледаше така: свирепите сили ја поставија својата дијагноза – градот е мртов во пет и седумнаесет.

О, човеку, ти што излезе од урнатините, од ужасот и грозотиите, ти што се искачи на врвот на невозможниот бол и ранет блесна со сета своја убавина, и ти што ги носиш во себе сите градови, сета мака нивна, сите соништа, сите надевања, ти што го запали својот бол со огнот на раѓањето – тебе ти ги давам овие редови, свесен за немоќта дека било кога тие ќе успеат да се допрат до длабината на твоето страдање, до силата на твојата благородност, до вишините на твојата неискажана човечка убавина.

Зашто овој град не се ни улиците ни плоштадите, липите и црвените каранфили, парковите и гулабите, кулите убави или грди, линиите на старата и новата архитектура што ја сече оваа Вардар река како човечка вододелница, како две страници од историјата. Зашто овој град не се овие гробишта од железо и бетон, од малтер и цигли, ни овие

Aco Šopov wrote the following text in late July or early August 1963, just days after the Skopje earthquake. It first appeared in Serbian in a Belgrade newspaper. The Macedonian version first appeared in the journal Sovremenost *13, nos. 7–8 (1963), pp. 425–427.*

AT FIVE SEVENTEEN

Someone has written: On the twenty-sixth day of July, in the year nineteen sixty-three, at five seventeen in the morning, the city on the Vardar died.

How terrible the verdict of nature, how catastrophic the peril of truth contained in that single moment of time—five seventeen. In the roar of the earth and the blocks of concrete—five seventeen. In the maelstrom of the buildings and the darkened sun—five seventeen. In the cry of the children whose dream, even beneath the rubble, could not flee the green fields of their eyes—five seventeen. In the strange silence of the mothers and fathers, the young men and young women, of those who, in a single moment, were left naked in the ashes of the demolished buildings, crushed beneath an inhuman freight of pain and suffering—five seventeen.

Five seventeen. Who can express in ordinary human words the drama of two hundred thousand inhabitants of this planet being pulled into the blind bowels of the earth—the drama of Five Seventeen?

Yes, that is how it appeared: cruel forces gave their diagnosis—the city died at five seventeen.

It is to you, who have emerged from the ruins, from the terror and the horrors; who have climbed to the summit of impossible pain and, wounded, shone forth in all your beauty; who carry all the cities within you, all their sorrows, all their dreams, all their hopes; who set your pain alight with the fire of birth—it is to you I give these lines, fully aware of their inability to ever touch the depth of your suffering, the strength of your nobility, the height of your unspoken human beauty.

For this city is not its streets and squares, its linden trees and red

темни заканувачки пукнатини на ѕидиштата, тие дијагонали на смртта, ни крововите што за чудо висат на тротоарите. Зашто овој град – тоа си ти, човеку. Зашто овој град – тоа е твојата невидена архитектура на совеста, љубовта, трпението и патилата, град на непознатата човечност во тебе.

Историјата ќе запише: градот на човечноста е роден во пет и седумнаесет.

Те гледав како го подигаш копајќи ги со нокти бетонските плочи за да го откриеш својот син, своето девојче, својот пријател, својот брат. Те гледав како се провлекуваш низ тесните пукнатини и дупки за да ги извлечеш од чељуста на пеколната неизвесност. Те гледав како со својот дах им го враќаш дахот на девојчињата и момчињата, обезличени од овој чудовишен судир на животот и смртта. Те гледав исцрпен, модар и премален од несон, од бдеење, од страдање над ранетите, над мртвите. Те гледав како ги повлекуваш границите на животот повеќе и над познатата човечка моќ и како на смртта ѝ одземаш дел по дел од нејзината власт. Те гледав врз урнатините, на патиштата, во збеговите, помеѓу возможноста и невозможноста.

Тој град се роди во пет и седумнаесет на она страотно утро кога земјата ревеше со ревот на уништувањето. Неговите кули на човечноста не се извишија во урбанистичките заводи, неговите улици на љубовта не се насликани на сликарските платна во затворени ателјеи, неговите домови на сочуство и човечко разбирање не се плод на трогателна поетска фантазија. Тој град на твојата нова човечност се роди во пет и седумнаесет.

Човеку, ти што излезе од урнатините, од ужасот и грозотиите ти што се искачи на врвот на болот, блесна со сета своја убавина и го запали сиот свој бол со огнот на раѓањето, те слушам како викаш:

„Поети, мајстори на зборот, архитекти на човечноста и солидарноста, исковете нови зборови за поимите на разбирањето и љубовта, помошта и братството, единството на човечките интереси, животот без страв и катастрофи. Во пет и седумнаесет е роден градот на иднината.”

carnations, its parks and pigeons, its towers both beautiful and ugly, the lines of its old and new architecture, which the Vardar River divides like a watershed between two pages of history. For this city is not these graves of iron and concrete, of mortar and brick, not these dark, menacing cracks in the walls, these diagonals of death, not these oddly suspended roofs above the sidewalks. For this city is you. This city is the invisible architecture of your conscience, your love, your patience and suffering, the city of the unrecognized humanity that lies within you.

History will write: The city of humanity was born at five seventeen.

I watched as you built it, your fingernails digging at the concrete slabs in search of your son, daughter, friend, brother. I watched as you crawled through narrow cracks and crevices to pull them from the jaws of hellish uncertainty. I watched as with your own breath you breathed life back into girls and boys disfigured by this monstrous clash of life and death. I saw you exhausted, pallid, and spent from sleeplessness, from keeping vigil, from grieving for the wounded, for the dead. I watched as you stretched the boundaries of life even beyond known human strength and bit by bit took power away from death. I watched you in the ruins, on the pathways, in the shelters, living between possibility and impossibility.

This city was born at five seventeen on that terrible morning when the earth roared with a roar of destruction. Its towers of humanity did not rise in institutes of urban planning; its streets of love were not painted on canvas in closed studios; its houses of compassion and human understanding are not the fruit of some touching poetic imagination. This city of your new humanity was born at five seventeen.

O you who emerged from the ruins, from the terror and the horrors, who climbed to the summit of pain, who shone forth in all your beauty and set your pain alight with the fire of birth, I hear you calling:

"Poets, masters of the word, architects of humanity and solidarity, forge new words for the concepts of understanding and love, of help and brotherhood, of the oneness of human concerns, of life without fear and disaster. At five seventeen the city of the future was born."

NOTES ON THE POEMS

Not-Being (1963) *(p. 3)*

Not-being is our attempt to translate Šopov's unusual word *nebidnina*, which he appears to have invented. See the introduction for more on this word, our translation of it, and the difficulty of pinpointing its meaning.

In this first section of our book, we present all the poems from Šopov's 1963 book *Not-Being* with one exception—"Romantic Flight" ["Romantič-no begstvo"], which Šopov excluded from *Scar* [*Luzna*] (1981), his last book of selected poems, which he himself compiled and organized. We have also made certain changes to the order of the poems: instead of opening immediately with the Prayer Cycle, we use the two poems "Down Below There Is a Blood" and "Scar" to lead the reader into Šopov's poetry. In this we again follow the 1981 collection, which opened with the same two poems.

Scar *(p. 7)*

elderwort – In Macedonian, *burjani*. Šopov is most likely referring to *Sambucus ebulus*, the flowering dwarf elder known in English by a number of traditional names, including *daneswort, walewort, blood hilder,* and *elderwort*.

Eighth Prayer of My Body, or, Who Will Conceive of That Love? *(p. 29)*

Svetlana Šopova, the poet's wife, recalls that her husband wrote this poem partly as a response to the first manned space flight by Yuri Gagarin on April 12, 1961. For the poet, this event changed forever humanity's relationship with the cosmos, in particular with the moon, which lost its romantic aura.

241

Rag-and-Bone Man *(p. 41)*

The Macedonian title is *Staro kupuvam,* which translates to "I buy old things." In the past, rag-and-bone men, usually Roma, would call this out as they went with a cart from neighborhood to neighborhood buying used clothes, scrap metal, and other household goods, which they would then resell. Even today their call can be heard (although less and less often) on the streets of Skopje and other Macedonian towns.

As published in the book *Not-Being,* the poem had four stanzas; when Šopov included the poem in *Scar,* however, he removed the two middle stanzas, possibly because he felt they introduced a comic tone that was out of place alongside the other *Not-Being* poems (in the 1963 book, the poem appeared in a separate section). Below, we provide a translation of the two missing stanzas, along with the original.

In the Macedonian poem—and especially in these middle stanzas—the voice of the rag-and-bone man is brought to life through the extensive use of words borrowed from Turkish, which had been the dominant language of government, culture, and the urban Muslim elite over the course of Macedonia's five-hundred-year rule by the Ottomans; it was also the language of many rural Muslim communities. After the Ottoman period, many of the Turkish words that had entered the Macedonian language disappeared, others became part of everyday use, while yet others became marked as colloquial or archaic but also intimate and familiar. It is this last layer of Turkish vocabulary that Šopov employs here, with great dexterity, to create the linguistic landscape of a vanishing era—nouns like *piskuli* ("tassels") and *eleci* ("vests"), adjectives like *kaleš* ("swarthy," here, "jet-eyed") and *ačik* ("open, clear"), verbs such as *bojadisa* ("paint, color," or here, with shoes, "polish"), interjections such as *aman* ("for mercy's sake!"), and expressions such as *tak-sa sebap* ("promise a favor"). While it was impossible to capture fully the rich texture of the rag-and-bone man's speech in our translation, we did our best to convey its compelling energy.

Here are the missing second and third stanzas:

Old things I buy and sell good as new.
Come on down, sir! Long life to your children!
Come down and rummage my empty pockets—you won't find as much as a buck.
Ah, if only you met our fine young bachelors!

If only you met Dalip, an ace of a guy,
you'd do him the goodness of offering your shoes,
and he'd take them and bow to you;
he'd resole them and polish them
till they shined like the morning sky.
And handsome, handsome, no one's more handsome!
He'd come down to the street in the neighborhood
so dashing and clear-eyed and all decked out,
and the girls, they'd be jostling each other,
and the women, exchanging such looks,
and the men, they'd be filled with envy.
Ah yes, old shoes—old things I buy!

Old things I buy and sell good as new.
For mercy's sake, dear lady (God be with you!),
why are you asking so much?
I'm a married man, with a wife and children,
long may the darlings live, but they've eaten me alive,
they've brought my house to rack and ruin!
This dress, now it really isn't your style—
here's a hundred dinars and let's call it even!
Ah, if only you knew our jet-eyed Kalina!
She's just getting ready to be a young bride.
How she will bless you! How she will thank you!
She'll bless your grandchildren, your great-grandchildren,
and all the generations yet to come!
Ah yes, old dresses for young brides—old things I buy!

Старо купувам, ново препродавам.
симни се, господине, жив ти дечињата,
да ми ја превртиш сета немаштија
нема да собереш една иљадарка.
Ех, да ги познаваш нашите ергени,
да си го вишол Далип најерген
ќе му ги таксаш себап чевлите.

Он ќе ги земе ќе ти се поклони,
ќе ги подзакрпи, ќе ги бојадиса,
па светнат како небо утринско
и личен, личен, нема поличен,
ќе слезе долу среде маало,
ќе слезе сербес, ачик, натокмен,
момите ќе се подбутнуваат,
жените ќе се огледуваат,
мажите ќе му завидуваат.
Ех, стари чевли, старо купувам.

Старо купувам, ново препродавам.
Аман, господарке, господ со тебе,
бива ли сега таква скапотија.
Женет сум, жена, деца сурија,
жив ми најмилото жив ме оглодаа,
куќата ми ја растурија.
Оваа риза не е за тебе,
еве ти стотка, речи аирлија.
Ех, да ја знаеш калеш Калина,
токму се токми млада невеста,
ќе ти се заблази, ќе ти благодари,
ќе ти благослови внуци и правнуци,
и сета челад од нивно колено.
Ех стари ризи млади невести.
старо купувам.

Nightfall (p. 49)

the shimmering, timid fish of your eyes – For the fish mentioned in this line,
Šopov uses the word *plašici*, the Macedonian name for a variety of bleak
(*Alburnus albidus alborella*) found in Lake Ohrid. Our translation aims
to suggest one of the principal qualities Macedonians associate with these
fish—their silvery gleam as they dart back and forth in schools just beneath
the water's surface—as well as the connotations of the word *plašici*, which is
related to *plašliv*: "timid, easily frightened."

The Fire's Love (p. 73)

To S. J. – The poem is dedicated to Šopov's friend, the poet and novelist Slavko Janevski (1920–2000), who, with Šopov and Blaže Koneski, was one of the founders of modern Macedonian poetry. Janevski and Šopov collaborated on several important publications, including the poetry collection *The Youth Railway* [*Pruga na Mladosta*] (1946) and their translation of the Russian poet Eduard Bagritsky's *The Lay of Opanas* (1951).

The Long Coming of the Fire (p. 75)

Šopov first presented the poem "The Long Coming of the Fire" on October 10, 1967, at the inauguration of the Macedonian Academy of Sciences and Arts. Earlier that year he and thirteen others had been elected as the first full members of the newly established academy. The poem was published first in the literary journal *Modernity* [*Sovremenost*] in March 1968, and then in the collection *The Golden Circle of Time* [*Zlaten krug na vremeto*] (1969). Although the other three Fire poems—"The Fire's Night," "The Fire's Retreat," and "The Fire's Love"—also appeared in this collection, they were not yet grouped together. It was only in 1970, with the publication of *Reader of the Ashes* [*Gledač vo pepelta*], that they appeared as a cycle. Later that year, in an interview for a newspaper, Šopov said of "The Long Coming of the Fire": "In it all my experience has, in a way, reached its highest achievement" ("Zagovornik na ljubovta, zemjata i strasta," interviewed by Cvetan Stanoevski, *Nova Makedonija*, November 28–29, 1970).

Beneath this wreath from sunheads wrought – The phrase translated as "sunheads"—*sončevi glavi*—very likely alludes to the Macedonian Partisans and civilians who were killed at the hands of the occupying Axis forces during World War II. It derives from the title of a poem by Blaže Koneski, "Sun Column" ["Sončeva kolona"] (1948), in which a group of slain Partisans are envisioned as marching in a column at dawn on a mountain ridge with the rising sun leading them onward. Šopov first borrowed Koneski's title for an essay in 1959, in which he described events he had seen as a Partisan fighter, and again, two years later, for the title of a short book that tells the story of twelve young men, one no older than fifteen, who were shot in cold blood near the village of Vataša by Bulgarian Army forces in June 1943: *The Twelve from the Sun Column of Youth* [*Dvanaestminata od sončevata kolona na mladosta*]—his only published book of prose.

Šopov's "wreath of sunheads" may well have inspired architect Bogdan Bogdanović's design of the Memorial Complex to Fallen Fighters for the Revolution, which is laid out on a hill overlooking the city of Štip, Šopov's hometown. The most striking feature of the memorial is a line of twelve marble cenotaphs, each with a unique spherical indentation that evokes a sun. In front of them stands a large marble pillar inscribed with eight lines from "The Long Coming of the Fire": the first and third couplets (which include the "sunheads" line) and the two couplets that end the poem.

Reader of the Ashes (group of poems) *(p. 85)*

Four of the eight poems in this group—"Horrordeath," "Lament from the Other Side of Life," "Tempest," and "August"—relate directly, if not explicitly, to the devastation of the earthquake that struck Skopje on July 26, 1963, in which over a thousand people died, several thousand were injured, and over a hundred thousand were left homeless. The other four poems—"The Golden Circle of Time," "If There Isn't Enough Light for You," "Night Spring," and "Reader of the Ashes"—which alternate in counterpoint with the earthquake-inspired poems, examine the poet's responsibility in the face of profound spiritual crisis.

Šopov addressed the earthquake most explicitly in the prose piece "At Five Seventeen" ["Vo pet i sedumnaeset"], which appeared soon after the tragedy in Serbian and Macedonian publications. We present a translation of this short text in the Appendix.

Horrordeath *(p. 87)*

The word *horrordeath* is a translation of the Macedonian *grozomor*, which Šopov invented by combining *groza* ("horror, dread") with the root *-mor-*, which relates to large-scale death; *pomor*, for example, means "slaughter, annihilation" as well as "plague."

snakeberry in the mouth – It is not clear what plant he is referring to by the word *zmijogrozd*, a compound from *zmij* ("snake") and *grozd* ("grape"). Some translators have interpreted this as veronica or arum. Our translation seeks to convey the ominous connotations of the Macedonian word, even if it is not botanically accurate. Coincidentally, "snakeberry" is a common English name used for the plant *Solanum dulcamara*, a member of the nightshade family that produces a bitter fruit that is, however, not as lethal as its more famous cousin, deadly nightshade.

Eyes *(p. 131)*

Along with the miniature "In Silence," "Eyes" is among Šopov's best-loved works. Generations of Macedonians learned it by heart at school, and even today many can recite the opening stanzas. The poet himself called it one of his favorite poems. He wrote it in Belgrade in 1945, and an early version appeared first in the literary journal *New Day* [*Nov den*] in 1946 and, almost immediately afterwards, in the important anthology *Poems* [*Pesni*], to which Koneski, Janevski, and two other poets also contributed. A somewhat revised version of the poem was then included in Šopov's collection *With Our Hands* [*So naši race*] (1950). The poem is dedicated to the memory of Šopov's first love, the Partisan fighter Vera Jocik (1923–1944), who served with the poet in the First Battalion of the Third Macedonian Shock Brigade. On May 20, 1944, she was gravely wounded in an attack on Bulgarian Army forces in the village of Stracin, in northern Macedonia. Her comrades pulled her out of the battle and carried her for three days and nights to another village, Sasa, where she died.

Beauty *(p. 137)*

To L. Ličenoski – The dedication is to Lazar Ličenoski (1901–1964), one of Macedonia's most important artists. He was part of the first generation of Macedonian painters who, after the tumultuous changes of the first decades of the twentieth century, strived to develop a contemporary Macedonian painting. Among his portraits is one of Aco Šopov painted in 1953.

I Seek My Voice (p. 145)

teeth of seed that sprout in the fields – Šopov is probably alluding to the Greek myth of Cadmus, who slayed a dragon and sowed its teeth in the ground, from which fierce armed men then sprang. Cadmus provoked them into attacking each other until only five were left standing. With these, he founded the city of Thebes. There are two reasons why Šopov may have been particularly interested in the Cadmus story: first, because Cadmus is credited with inventing the alphabet, and, second, because he is said to have journeyed in his later years to Illyria, where he founded the city of Lychnidos—today known as Ohrid, on the lake of that name in Macedonia.

The Song of the Black Woman (1976) (p. 185)

The poems in *The Song of the Black Woman* [*Pesna na crnata žena*] were written during Šopov's tenure as the Yugoslav ambassador to Senegal, from 1971 to 1975. Many are inspired by, and in dialogue with, the work of Léopold Sédar Senghor (1906–2001), a renowned poet and one of the founders of the Négritude movement, who was also the first president of Senegal (from 1960 to 1980). Šopov translated a large selection of Senghor's poems for the collection *Poezija* [*Poetry*] (1975).

In a 1978 newspaper interview, Šopov described how his years in Africa had affected his poetry: "Once a person has come to know and feel the rhythm of Black Africa, the wild call of the savanna and the virgin forest, it is hard to be free of those mysterious noises and cries." As a result of this influence, he explains, his verse line became "more elastic, broader, more pliable to the call of Africa." He goes on to say that in his book he has tried "to sort out my impressions from Black Africa, although in fact I am sorting out my impressions of my homeland." ("Granice slobode su granice stvaralaštva," interviewed by Nenad Radanović, *Oslobođenje*, October 14, 1978.)

Visually, the book is one of Šopov's most striking publications. It was designed by Niko Tozi, with large, often whole-page, sepia-toned photographs of African art interspersed among the poems. These dramatic images of sculptures and masks, taken by photographer Robert Jaki in a way that emphasizes their shadows, seem to illustrate Senghor's ideas about the aesthetic aspect of Négritude, in which African art was meant to convey not the visible reality, but the "sub-reality" of the underlying vital forces.

Into the Black Woman's Dream *(p. 189)*

Šopov's evocation of the beauty and allure of Africa through the image of the body of the Black woman may, to some degree, be read as a response to Senghor's famous poem "Black Woman" ["Femme noire"] (1945).

you are the song of songs – An allusion to the Biblical book The Song of Songs, which is constructed as a passionate dialogue between two lovers, King Solomon and the Shulammite, who says of herself: "I am black, but comely" (1:5).

Before the Flamboyants Bloomed *(p. 193)*

The *flamboyants* of the title are tropical flowering trees—*Delonix regia*, also known as *royal poinciana*—which line the streets of Dakar. They grow up to forty feet and have a wide, umbrella-like canopy of feathery leaves. When they blossom, they produce a magnificent display of large, bright red flowers, signaling the end of the gray, dusty dry season and the city's return to life.

Woman in the Rainy Season *(p. 197)*

hivernage – In Francophone West Africa, including Senegal, the French word *hivernage* refers not, as one might expect, to winter, but to the rainy season from July to September, which is characterized by severe storms and torrential rains. Šopov Macedonizes the French word as *ivernaž*, which he uses throughout the poem, including in the title.

The Light of the Slaves *(p. 207)*

In *The Song of the Black Woman*, this poem was presented as a single work with five separate parts—just as we present it here. In the 1981 *Scar* collection, however, the poem appeared with only four parts, while the fifth, "In the Eyes of the Signares," was formatted as a separate poem. It is difficult to believe that this truncation, which destroys the poem's clear integrity, was an intentional decision on the poet's part; more likely, it was a printing error. Nevertheless, the mistake was repeated in later editions of Šopov's work, including, for instance, the most recent substantial edition of his poetry in Macedonian, *The Birth of the Word* [*Raǵanjeto na zborot*] (2008), edited by Katica Ḱulavkova, where only the truncated version of the poem appeared. We are happy that we can present the poem in its entirety here.

like northern Signares – See the note below.

House of Slaves – Šopov is alluding to a building on **Gorée** (mentioned later in the poem), an island about a mile off the coast of Dakar that was a major slave-trading center from the fifteenth to the early-nineteenth century. Known today as the House of Slaves (*Maison des Esclaves*) the building was built in 1776 by a wealthy Franco-African slave-trading family. Enslaved people were kept locked in cells under horrific conditions before being put on the ships that would carry them to the Americas. In 1962, the house was renovated and opened as a museum about the slave trade and as a memorial to its victims.

the Lighthouse of the Mamelles – A strategically important lighthouse, built in 1864, which stands on the higher of two hills known as *les Mamelles* ("the Breasts") on Cap Vert, the westernmost point of Africa, in Dakar.

arrayed like princes of Mali – Šopov is referring to the Mali Empire, which existed from the early thirteenth to the late seventeenth century. At its greatest extent, it reached from the Atlantic coast of Senegal and Gambia to the upper stretches of the Niger River. Šopov's image is borrowed from Senghor's "Black Woman," where it similarly evokes the noble beauty of the African people.

the Land of the Dogons – Also called Dogon Country (in French, *Pays Dogon*), this is a vast region in eastern Mali and northeastern Burkina Faso inhabited by the Dogon people.

their chosen Signare – The Signares (a word derived from the Portuguese title *senhora*) were women of mixed race born to local African women and European traders. Although the history of the Signares is complex—many were themselves wealthy traders in gold, ivory, and slaves—in this poem (and two others, not translated here, from *The Song of the Black Woman*) they are idealized as fine ladies of great beauty and elegance, able to wield power over the hearts of men. Šopov very likely borrowed this image of the Signares from Senghor's *Chants pour Signares* (published in *Nocturnes*, 1961).

ABOUT THE CONTRIBUTORS

Aco Šopov was born in 1923 in the city of Štip in what is today North Macedonia. His first book was published by the underground press near the end of World War II, in which he had fought as a Partisan in the anti-fascist resistance. By the early 1950s, he was a major Macedonian poet. His books *Not-Being* (*Nebidnina*, 1963) and *Reader of the Ashes* (*Gledač vo pepelta*, 1970) are genuine masterworks, consolidating his reputation as one of the founders of modern Macedonian poetry. Šopov's poetic mission was to develop a poetry rooted in his own culture and language that is also universal and modern, and to do this not by turning away from tradition but by drawing on something that is both of the moment yet beyond the realm of time. This creative yet destructive impulse, which lies at the core of being, he called "the fire." His health began to decline in the late 1970s, and he died in 1982, at the age of fifty-eight. Šopov's work has been translated into over a dozen languages. This bilingual collection, which marks the poet's centennial, is the first major edition of Šopov's poetry in English.

Jasmina Šopova, a journalist, translator, and editor, was until recently the longtime editor-in-chief of the quarterly magazine *The UNESCO Courier*, where she published articles and interviews with Enki Bilal, René Depestre, Édouard Maunick, Predrag Matvejević, and other writers and artists from France, the Caribbean, Africa, and Southeastern Europe. She has translated the poets Adonis and Mahmoud Darwish from French into Macedonian and the Macedonian poets Ante Popovski, Vlada Uroševik, and Aco Šopov (her father) into French. She is the author of a number of monographs and critical editions in the field of poetry. As the vice-president of the Aco Šopov Poetry Foundation, she manages the foundation's multilingual website devoted to her father's life and work (www.acosopov.com).

Rawley Grau is best known as a translator from Russian and Slovenian. His translation of the Russian poet Yevgeny Baratynsky (*A Science Not for the Earth*, 2015) received the AATSEEL Prize for Best Scholarly Translation and was listed by *Three Percent* as one of the ten best poetry translations of the year. His translations from Slovenian of two novels by Dušan Šarotar (*Panorama*, 2017, and *Billiards at the Hotel Dobray*, 2019) were shortlisted for the Oxford-Weidenfeld Prize. In 2021, he was awarded the Lavrin Diploma for excellence in translation by the Slovenian Association of Literary Translators. Originally from Baltimore, he has lived in Ljubljana, Slovenia, since the early 2000s.

Christina E. Kramer is a professor emerita at the University of Toronto, Canada, where she taught Macedonian for more than thirty years. She is the author of numerous articles on Balkan linguistics as well as a Macedonian grammar. Her translations include *Fear of Barbarians* by Petar Andonovski (Parthian Press, 2022); *A Spare Life* by Lidija Dimkovska (Two Lines Press, 2016, longlisted for Best Translated Book of the year); *Freud's Sister* by Goce Smilevski (Penguin Books, 2012, Lois Roth Prize Honourable Mention); and three novels by Luan Starova: *My Father's Books* and *The Time of the Goats* (both University of Wisconsin Press, 2012), and *The Path of the Eels* (supported by an NEA grant; Autumn Hill Books, 2017). For additional information: www.christinakramertranslator.ca.

Printed in the USA
CPSIA information can be obtained
at www.ICGtesting.com
JSHW030307170823
46715JS00002B/6

9 781646 053032